AF725770

Praise for
Welcoming Our Gods Back Home

No one collects old light bulbs after the light has gone out, but we tend to hang on to the formative images of our history and wonder why they are no longer numinous to us. In this book, Jungian analyst Jerry Wright reminds us that all encounters, all, are experienced within, and explores our complicity in the formation of religious images and concepts. The ultimate otherness of the Other, what many have called God, obliges us to track how these images rise in us, are framed by our human equipment, and thus speak more of our psychologies than point one to the mystery. Nonetheless, he notes that our openness to the numinosity all about us, within us, opens the modern to encounter the mysteries anew.

- **James Hollis, Ph.D.**, is a Jungian analyst, author of many books including *Tracking the Gods: The Place of Myth in Modern Life.*

Presbyterian pastor and Jungian analyst Jerry Wright takes us on a reflective journey exploring the death of the monotheistic myth of "Father," living outside of the psyche, as a projection of shadow. Beginning with a description of the current political godhead that is instilling fear through a misuse of power, Wright moves beyond internalized god-images into psychological mysticism. He invites us into experiencing a felt-sense of divine encounter, offering a unifying framework for envisioning the potential for a shared religious, cultural, and political future.

- **Deborah Bryon, Ph.D.**, Jungian analyst, and author of *Time and Trauma in Analytical Psychology and Psychotherapy: The Wisdom of Andean Shamanism.*

We live in perilous times. We have never been in greater need of a rigorous and inspiring spiritual wisdom to ground our life together. This book provides guidance for those seeking an authentic spiritual life that integrates all we have learned from the scientific disciplines of depth psychology, biology, and cosmology. Wright accesses the powerful archetypal energies present in every human psyche, while avoiding the limitations of pre-modern world views. Here is a path for those seeking a deepening spiritual encounter with the awe and wonder of the universe but have been stymied by religious doctrine and dogma. Intellectually satisfying and spiritually inspiring, this book provides guidance for the modern mystic.

- **Allen Proctor, M. Div.**, Director Emeritus, The Haden Institute.

In a world disconnected from the transformative power of wisdom traditions reduced to mere systems of belief and belonging, Dr. Wright once again speaks new life over dry bones. Welcoming Our Gods Back Home welcomes us back to the numinosity of direct experience, to relating to the unspeakable within us and between us. With his usual candor and deep insight, Dr. Wright has written a true cri du coeur, calling each reader to the sacred tasks of reclamation and re-ensoulment in a world desacralized by mere religion.

- **Tony Caldwell, M.S.W., L.C.S.W.**, Jungian analyst, faculty member of The Haden Institute.

Grounded in psychological integrity, scientific honesty, and a deeply religious attitude, Welcoming Our Gods Back Home is a valuable read for those who long to read through the current chaos with hope, who long for ways of realizing our interconnected relationships to all things, and who desire to deepen relationships with the gods who are truly closer than we dare to imagine. Dr. Jerry Wright invites us to consider that the divisions between us are much smaller than the current chaos would have us feel and believe. Written with the keen insight of one who has consciously faced the difficult questions of life and religion, the book is a celebration of the human spirit, and it left me with a renewed trust in our shared future.

- **Cari Keith, BSN, M.Div.**, former Director of The Guild for Spiritual Guidance, pilgrimage leader.

WELCOMING OUR GODS BACK HOME

The Wisdom of Psychological Mysticism

Volume Three of the Trilogy
Jungian Psychology and the Future of Our Species

JERRY R. WRIGHT
Jungian Psychoanalyst

CHIRON PUBLICATIONS • ASHEVILLE, NORTH CAROLINA

© 2025 by Chiron Publications. All rights reserved. No part of this publication may be reproduced, stored in a retrieval system, or transmitted, in any form by any means, electronic, mechanical, photocopying, recording, or otherwise, without the prior written permission of the publisher, Chiron Publications, P.O. Box 19690, Asheville, N.C. 28815-1690.

This work may not be used without permission for artificial intelligence training or development of machine learning language models.

www.ChironPublications.com

Interior and cover design by Danijela Mijailovic
Printed primarily in the United States of America.

ISBN 978-1-68503-660-7 paperback
ISBN 978-1-68503-661-4 hardcover
ISBN 978-1-68503-662-1 electronic
ISBN 978-1-68503-663-8 limited edition paperback
ISBN 978-1-68503-664-5 limited edition hardcover

Library of Congress Cataloging-in-Publication Data Pending

Dedicated
to my teachers, mentors, and psychoanalysts
who have served as
mirrors and icons
for my life and work ...

And to Harriett Richie and Susan Smartt
who with keen eyes and generous hearts
read, read, and reread
the manuscripts for this trilogy.

We live our lives in widening circles
that reach out across the world.
We may not complete this last one
but we give ourselves to it.

We circle around the great mysteries.
We have been circling for thousands of years
and we still don't know:
Are we creatures, or humans, or pure soul?
We only know that we are on our way home.
(Wright, inspired by poems from Rilke's *Book of Hours*)

WELCOMING OUR GODS BACK HOME
The Wisdom of Psychological Mysticism

PREFACE

From his rich depth psychological perspective, Swiss psychiatrist Carl Gustav Jung proposed that the birthplace of all of our deities and devils has been, and will be, the human psyche and imagination. This perspective provides a radical, and necessary, correction to long-held religious perspectives and religious delusions.

For many centuries and countless generations, our species has studied religions, sacred texts, and religious dogma, while seeking to understand the character and will of external, supernatural beings to whom we have given countless names and dwelling places. This seeking is the passionate work of *theology*. For the last century, a mere three generations, many people have studied the same religions and their documents while seeking to understand the nature, dynamics, and the active and latent capacities of the human psyche. This study is the passionate work of *depth psychology*, or the psychology of the unconscious, particularly the Analytical Psychology of Carl Gustav Jung.

For the first half of my life, I looked through a theological lens to make meaning of my life and the life of the world around and beyond me. For the second half of my life, my preferred eyeglass has been the depth psychological lens as I have sought to integrate the two perspectives.

Welcoming Our Gods Back Home: The Wisdom of Psychological Mysticism continues my passionate pursuit of the mysteries we are to ourselves as we contemplate our place and role in the mysterious, numinous universe. This third volume completes the trilogy *Jungian Psychology and the Future of Our Species*. Brief summaries of my first two volumes appear later in this preface. Both are available through Chiron Publications and Amazon.

This third volume was inspired by the following dream on February 3, 2024, the day after Groundhog Day. The dream:

> *I am in a seminar setting with 30-40 participants. The leader is seated behind me and to the left. I sense his presence—a familiar stranger, a composite of several of my teachers and mentors.*
>
> *There is a pause in the conversation, and suddenly I feel compelled to speak. I say that I want to make a confession about my worldview and spiritual perspective. I refer to the two books I have authored. I note that many readers consider them to be too radical concerning the theistic and monotheistic images of God, as well as concerning religion in general. I confess that today I think they are <u>too tame</u> and <u>not radical enough</u> for what is needed.*
>
> *I acknowledge that I am narcissistic to think I have anything to say about the Divine and about the mysteries of life and my place and role in those mysteries. Yet, I excuse my writing by suggesting that all writers have a strain of narcissism. Otherwise, they would never publish anything. I elaborate on this notion and declare that I feel compelled to keep writing and speaking about the unspeakable, especially about the notion that all of our gods and religions have been birthed through and by the human psyche and imagination. I say, "Of course, this is the opposite of the common, historical view that we are birthed by an eternal, transcendent, supernatural, interventionist Being that we have named God. I declare, "So be it!"*

On awakening, I recall the dream and its major images before reaching for my journal. Once again, as the case has been for many years, I awake within minutes of 4 a.m. with the familiar urge to wonder about, to write about, and to speak about the mysteries in which we find ourselves. Suddenly, I remember that today is the day after Groundhog Day, and I remember one of my favorite movies.

"Groundhog Day" is a classic movie. I never tire of watching it. I see something new each time. I thoroughly identify with the comic weatherman, Phil Collins, played by Bill Murray. Morning after morning he wakes at 6 a.m. and repeats the same routines as he prepares to report on Punxsutawney Phil, the mystical groundhog who foretells the date of spring by whether or not he sees his shadow. Of course, spring always begins six weeks after February 2, groundhog shadow or not. But never mind. The whole exercise is a wonderful annual cultural ritual set in the state of Pennsylvania and followed by many in other states. Canada has its own version of the groundhog ritual as devotees observe the shadow of Shubenacadie Sam, otherwise known as Groundhog Sam.

The movie also contains much psychological and spiritual wisdom. It portrays the transformation of weatherman Phil, a patriarchal, narcissistic, know-it-all. His transformation is fueled by his initial lust for, and eventual love for, his coworker Rita. She is played by another favorite actress, Andie MacDowell. Step by step, day after day, Phil's lust gives way to falling in love and eventually learning how to love. It is the familiar pattern of Western romance, which, when it runs its complete course, can be a beautiful and sacred experience. Yes, it is another point of personal identification with the iconic movie!

So, I awoke on February 3 with the desire to keep circling the mysteries, beginning this time with the heretical notion that *it is we who birth all our gods rather than being birthed by them.* This is more than a turn of phrase. It has the potential to turn the monotheistic God-image and religion upside down and outside in. For me, it is a necessary turning, and it is long overdue.

My first two books address this urgent need for our species and our beautiful nest. Taken together, the three volumes provide the reader with an introduction to the Analytical Psychology of Carl Gustav Jung, especially with his concern for the recovery of soul in all aspects of life, including religion. The trilogy also provides an introduction to *psychological mysticism,* an interim psychospiritual paradigm as we await a new collective myth. The three volumes are also part of my personal and professional testament, a kind of memoir. The volumes bear witness to my lifelong search for meaning that combines religion and depth psychology.

I am reminded of a quip attributed to E. B. White: *I awake in the morning torn between the desire to improve the world and the desire to simply enjoy the world. This makes it hard to plan the day.* I know my version of those dueling desires. In the face of so many conflicts, political divisions, and repeated traumas, I am often tempted to give in to cynicism and apathy, to give up trying to improve the world, and to live my remaining days in imagined comfort with no concern for others beyond my little tribe. So far, I have resisted this tantalizing temptation. Readers may recognize their version of this modern struggle, especially during these politically trying times.

Before introducing the contents of the present volume, here are brief summaries of my first two books.

Volume One, *Reimagining God and Religion: Essays for the Psychologically Minded* (Chiron 2018), provides an introduction to the Analytical Psychology of C. G. Jung, commonly referred to as Jungian Psychology. The essay "Dreams: Strangers in the Night," highlights the special role of dreamwork in the individuation process. This essay is a resource for those who are beginning to pay attention to their dreams, as well as for dreamwork veterans. Special attention is given to the little-known dynamics and role of *psychological projection* that underlie all human relationships, as well as all god-images and religions. Critical attention is granted the three monotheistic religions—Judaism, Christianity, and Islam and their collective pathology that I identified as *Monotheistic Madness.* Included is a thorough examination of the difference between the historical Jesus of Nazareth and the universal, mystical image of Christ. Finally, two critical endeavors are proposed for the thriving (perhaps even surviving) of our species: (1) to gradually eulogize, bury, and grieve the theistic and monotheistic images of God and the religions dependent on them; and (2) to bring fresh imagination to the meanings of *god* and *religion* that can speak to the modern mind and ancient soul.

Volume Two, *A Mystical Path Less Traveled: A Jungian Psychological Perspective* (Chiron 2021), provides the foundation for a *psychological mysticism* that preceded and now replaces traditional *theological mysticism,* which was dependent on theistic images of God that are no longer relevant as I proposed in Volume One. Volume Two expands the meaning of mystic and mystical and validates the universality of human experiences of the *numinous,* a key foundation stone of Jung's psychological house. Drawing on Jung's psychology, on various mystical traditions, and on the exciting discoveries of modern sciences, *A Mystical Path Less Traveled* locates the sacred within Nature, within matter, within the human psyche— rather than outside or beyond. Psychological mysticism seeks to overcome the multiple dualisms in traditional God-images and religions, and to promote the perspective that the whole of life is a mystical sanctuary.

This third volume, *Welcoming Our Gods Back Home: The Wisdom of Psychological Mysticism*, extends the meanings of psychological mysticism as a transitional or bridge myth between the earlier religious, political, and cultural paradigms that have lost their capacity to mediate meaning, and a new collective myth that struggles to be born. Many reflective leaders and writers are speaking to this liminal, in-between time for our species, and are offering religious, cultural, and political perspectives. To these important perspectives, I add the perspective of Analytical Psychology that provides an indispensable depth dimension to the conversations.

The book title proposes that our modern psychospiritual task will require retrieving our deities and devils from their external domains and bringing them back home to the human psyche and imagination, where they originated and where they belong. Then, and likely only then, can we claim responsibility for our creative and destructive capacities we formerly assigned to external beings. Until then, the divisions, destructions, and deaths that we visit on each other, and on our Earth home, will likely continue and increase.

This final volume of my trilogy can be considered an extended commentary on the first two volumes. It includes my further wonderings and reflections as I wrestle, Jacob-like, with the mysteries that remain unnamable and, I believe, are ultimately unknowable by human consciousness. Nevertheless, we are not exempt from a lifetime of intense searching and reflection that gives way to awe and wonder, the two fruits of faith. I bow to the poet Rilke's observation that in wrestling with the angels "we grow by being defeated, decisively, by ever greater powers," by ever greater mysteries (Bly 1981:105-06).

The trilogy lays out a possible future for religion and spirituality which overcomes the divisive tribalism that has been the history of our species. Finding a path beyond toxic, religious tribalism may be our most important individual and collective task because religious tribalism contaminates all aspects of life and all people. This contamination happens unconsciously whether or not we consider ourselves to be religious or spiritual. Beneath our multiple political and cultural divisions lurks a religious shadow that grows darker with each generation of neglect. Unless and until we bring that individual and collective religious shadow to the light of consciousness, we will continue to do great harm to ourselves, to each other, and to our nest. This urgent refrain is echoed throughout the trilogy.

For the "Introduction" to this third volume, I have chosen to include significant portions of the "Afterword" of Volume One. It includes important autobiographical references, including reflections on a pivotal dream that metaphorically marked the first half of my life and the beginning of the second half. That dream is also a key part of Chapter Four of this volume. I hope that including portions of the earlier volume will provide clarity and continuity, especially for readers who may not have access to it.

The initial chapter in this third installment, "Speaking to the Political Elephant in the Room," addresses our current urgent national and worldwide crisis, a crisis that portends to be with us for many years. That elephant cannot be avoided as we seek to navigate our *collective dark night of the soul.* The essay identifies the characteristic of a cult and cult leaders, and suggests that the administration of President Donald J. Trump operates as a political cult with religious validation, the deadliest variety. Then, widening the critique and looking through a depth psychological lens, the essay identifies the fears that contribute to the dysfunction of all political parties, as well as to each and all of us. Finally, the essay calls for the recognition, withdrawal, and integration of the personal *shadow* as the one best gift we can offer each other. It is potentially the brightest light we have to navigate our *collective dark night of the soul.*

The final section of this volume, "Psychological Mysticism in Verse," includes poems by the author that were first published as "Trailmarkers" in Volume Two. Some have been slightly revised.

This book combines the writing styles of the first two volumes, a combination of brief journal entries and longer narratives or essays around various themes related to the title. Once again, I encourage what I call *magnetic reading* that reflects my own reading preference at this stage of my life. Except for novels, I seldom read new books cover to cover. Rather, with my journal at my side, I read a new book or article until something within me stirs awake as if desiring expression. Then, I lay the book or article aside, open my journal, and record what bubbles forth. This is what I mean by magnetic reading, sometimes called deep reading.

You are invited to read with your own journal in hand. The contents preserved therein will be your most valuable, and most authoritative, resource for your own path.

NOTES TO READERS

- When writing or speaking in public, I like to remind myself, and others, that I write and speak primarily as a Jungian Psychoanalyst who also has a background in theology. I am offering depth psychological perspectives on multiple disciplines, including theology.
- For all the reasons expressed in these pages, I rarely use the traditional word *God* except when referring to the theistic God-image of monotheism. I prefer to use

other metaphors such as Sacred Source, Wisdom, and Ultimate Reality. My use of the noncapitalized *god* and *gods* is a psychological designation. They refer to *internal, intrapsychic images, energies, and resources,* rather than external theistic beings. Depending on the context, *god* and *gods* include what we designate as creative and destructive forces, or good and evil.

- Frequent references to volumes one and two of this trilogy are noted with my last name, date of publication, and page number. For example, to reference some passage in Volume One, *Reimagining God and Religion*, it will be noted as (Wright 2018:00).
- The epigrams that appear in some of the chapter headings are my renderings of poems by Rainer Maria Rilke. The renderings were inspired by the translations of the same poems by Anita Barrows and Joanna Macy in *Rilke's Book of Hours: Love Poems to God,* pages 88, 119, 121. See Sources Cited.
- References to the *Collected Works of C. G. Jung* will appear as paragraph numbers, except when specifically designated as page numbers.

INTRODUCTION

I had a dream. I have a dream.

I had a dream that I took to my first Jungian analyst a half-lifetime ago when I was 38. It was an initial dream that often speaks to the major issues and complexes that are seeking consciousness. Initial dreams often lay out the psychological contours of a Jungian analysis, although those contours are initially unseen, even unimaginable to the dreamer. Analysts may carefully, reverently, hold the initial dream(s) of their clients in their consciousness while watching for how and when their meanings may be revealed. The dream's mysterious manifestation and meanings are initially hidden from the analyst, as well. The dream:

> My father has died, and we are standing beside the casket at the gravesite. A disembodied voice announces that there cannot be a burial until an autopsy is performed. I reach for the casket to brush off some ice/snow around the edges while asking, "Is this okay?" The voice replies, "Sure."

The size or length of a dream has little to do with its significance. Brief dreams may have enormous existential value and multiple meanings that continue to reveal themselves for many years. Such is the case here. The dream remains alive to this day and will likely continue to be a source of revelation.

In retrospect, the second half of my psychological life has been an autopsy of the death of my *father* in the many meanings of that *complex* identity. My biological father had died a decade before this dream. He was the oldest of 12 siblings, a hard worker and good provider. Emotionally distant except for regular outbursts of anger growing out of his own frustrations, he expressed his love by faithful attendance at my sports endeavors from childhood through college. He was only 52 when he died of lung cancer. He died just before I was emotionally ready to reconnect with him as a young father myself. The early part of my analysis involved grieving that primary relationship, including brushing off the ice and snow, which was symbolic of our emotional relationship. It was also a wake-up call to be more emotionally available to my own three children. As parents, we may repeat how we were parented or go to the other extreme declaring we will be just the opposite, thereby falling in the opposite ditch. Or, with the hard work of consciousness, we can choose something different that fits with our own personality and desires. Parental complexes, both father and mother, frequently occupy the first stages of psychoanalysis and get recycled throughout. The autopsy of the historical and personal father, and my own parenting as a father, continue to this day.

In my professional life as a Presbyterian pastor and Jungian analyst, I have been privileged to serve as a *spiritual and/or psychological father* to many, with a mixture of satisfaction and some inevitable regrets. The helping professions often attract those who need help themselves. That attraction can be doubled-edged. On the one hand, attending to the needs of others can be an escape from tending our own. On the other hand, our mistakes and missteps can force us into therapy and/or analysis. Some of us become analysts because we need so much analysis! The prospective nature of my dream suggested that a continuing examination, a continuing autopsy, of the ever-changing role as pastor, and later as a Jungian analyst, would be required.

One further autopsy has motivated and necessitated this writing project, and in many ways, it remains the most significant at this stage of my life. Unknown and unforeseen by me at the time, yet apparently clear to the unconscious, the dream anticipated the death for me of the images *Father God* or *Heavenly Father*, including the inevitable grieving and the necessary autopsy. In the essay "Beyond the Back Porch of the Church," I acknowledge the unconscious grief that had symptomized in anger and loss of meaning prior to leaving the sanctuary and the safety of the Church. The ice and snow on the casket were symbolic of the lack of warmth that traditional religious structures and interpretations were providing. For me they had become cold, frozen, and rigid.

In retrospect, the last half of my life has been directed by the scary and sacred autopsy of the death of the monotheistic myth with its core image of an external, metaphysical, interventionist, divine *Father*. The preliminary autopsy report includes the following:

> With the necessary demise and death of antique cosmologies and traditional religious paradigms dependent on external supernatural deities and devils, the modern religious challenge involves two simultaneous sacred endeavors: to eulogize, bury, and grieve the theistic and monotheistic god-images and the religious paradigms dependent on them; and secondly, to bring fresh imagination to the meanings of *god* and *religion* that will satisfy both the modern mind and ancient soul (Wright 2018:191).

Autopsies are performed for numerous reasons. In all cases, they are for the benefit of the living rather than for the deceased.

They may provide critical information about the cause of death, which may be helpful to the grieving. They may provide research information that can assist the living in terms of quantity and quality of life. They can provide information about *what was* in order to imagine *what could be.* Physical autopsies are about examining the past in order to be helpful to the present and to anticipate the future. Religious autopsies may perform a similar function, which brings me to my dream of our religious future.

I have a dream. Metaphorically, this dream originates in the future and approaches humanity over the distant horizon. Nighttime dreams emerge from the mysterious depths of life, and this dream approaches us from the far evolutionary horizon. Ordinarily, we think of the future as an extension of the past coming through the present. Yet, we can also imagine we meet the future as it comes toward us from beyond the horizon, a future inviting human consciousness and needing human consciousness to manifest, to materialize. This perspective is an extension of Jung's far-reaching intuition that divinity needs human consciousness to become conscious of itself. To entertain that possibility, one has to get beyond the theistic and monotheistic god-image, which these essays propose has lost its meaning and its evolutionary role. It requires that we bring fresh imagination to the meanings of god and religion if we are to move beyond our divisive, tribal religions to embrace inclusive, global ones. This is the future of which I dream.

As I scan the distant religious horizon, my dream is for religions that will be inclusive, intellectually and scientifically honest, and soul-satisfying. They will be free from imagined external deities and devils. They will build bridges rather than walls, however defined. In the meantime, the unconscious grieving of the death of theism and monotheism will continue with its attendant individual and collective pathos. My psychological conclusion: *As long as our deities and devils are perceived to be beyond the physical world and outside the human psyche, we will continue to do great harm to ourselves, to each other, and to our nest.*

The fertile marriage of unconscious and conscious has the potential to birth new images of *god* and *religion*. My hope is that our species will eventually embrace the psychological conclusion that it is the human imagination that creates god-images and religions, drawing from a metapersonal storehouse of accumulated wisdom. Jung calls this storehouse the collective unconscious. The language to describe these creative mysteries will likely evolve, yet the conclusion seems inevitable. Thus far, theistic and monotheistic religions have outsourced what is best and worst about our species. The religion of the future will facilitate the retrieval of our capacities for great good and great evil so that we will have some measure of choice about which to incarnate.

Looking back from a place far down the evolutionary road, we may see the religions of the past as necessary stages along a twisting, labyrinthine path toward the realization that *we are, in fact, what we imaged our former deities and devils to be.* No, we will not see ourselves as little gods. Rather, we will accept our full humanity through whom both godly and demonic powers are manifest. Our species will conclude that, in the wisdom of psyche, it was necessary to see our creative and destructive capacities in projected form until we could own them and manifest both responsibly. We will come to recognize and to own both our glory and gory, which were projected, necessarily so, onto external deities and devils. Squinting, that is as far as I can see.

The realization of the potentials our species once deemed divine will have little resemblance, however, to the illusory super race or superman syndrome that grew out of the Enlightenment.

The antidote to religious or psychological inflation will be the ready reminder of our individual and collective shadow, our capacity for destruction. This dark reminder will light our path forward.

Until we can collectively own that darkness, my immediate concern is whether our species can survive and thrive. To be religiously and psychologically honest, we need to acknowledge that our species may well self-destruct, although the cosmic drama played long before our arrival will continue. The universe did not come into being solely to meet our species' narcissistic needs, nor does it need our species to continue. That may be a hard religious pill to swallow. We have created massive numbers of instruments of our suicide, instruments not-so-safely stored underground, while we spend an inordinate amount of international concern trying to keep more deadly instruments out of the hands of our competitors. Of course, as the world's superpower, we maintain the illusion that we, and we only, are capable of using the instruments of suicide wisely and responsibly. Yet, we are the world's chief supplier of armaments. As I discussed in an earlier essay, technological information is not synonymous with consciousness. At present, we do not have the collective *psychological technology* necessary for our long-term survival as a species. This was Jung's chief concern. The same concern has fueled this writing.

Paradoxically for Western culture that worships at the altars of progress, our future may well depend on coming to terms with our *finitude* rather than trusting in *plenitude*. Our relationship with limits, mortality, and death must replace our worship of abundance, progress, and eternal life. This will be an arduous political and religious undertaking. Many of our daily concerns are First World worries—

my cellphone is not getting good reception, the warning light in my car has come on, my suit or dress is out of style, etc.

Collectively, we judge a good day by whether the stock market is up or down. We are a nation of plenty, with plenty of people in dire straits kept out of sight, even as we try to keep our concerns about our aging, our mortality, our sure and certain death out of sight. Those individual delusions are multiplied in our collective refusal to look at climate change, world hunger, the growing gap between wealth and poverty, and our suicidal relationship with armaments of all shapes and sizes. A further delusion casts these human issues as political rather than religious; we prefer to keep our religious life, and hands, sanitized.

Many years ago, one of my mentors, Quaker John Yungblut, offered wise counsel as he engaged us on retreat and as he engaged his own health concerns, advanced Parkinson's disease. Without blame or self-pity, he said that his current religious task was learning "to hallow my diminishments." It is a phrase whose meaning I will always remember: to *make holy* his decline, his limitations, his mortality, his impending death. He was speaking about his individual situation but he speaks for all of us. No one has gotten out of this life alive, although we all think at some level we will be the exception. How do we hallow this life in all its glory and gory rather than run from it with hollow pursuits? How do we claim our connection with all rather than competing as if we have unlimited time and resources? What does it mean to be number one if we are no longer around to do a victory dance? As part of my dream, the religions of the future will need to help us live this mortal life fully, passionately, and compassionately rather than promise eternal life and a heavenly reward. Life may well continue in some form since the energy of which we are made never ceases but transforms; however, that possible form lies beyond the reach of our imagination. I have yet to hear a view of heaven that sounds inviting, although I am open to being surprised.

While expressing his concern for our future, Jung remained hopeful, as do I. Half of that hope lies in the power of consciousness itself, the capacity of individuals to be the conduits of the resources of the deep springs of life itself. Small as our individual advancements in consciousness may be—akin to placing an infinitesimal grain of sand on the scale of humanity's soul—we would do well to assume that our small offering may tip the scale toward wholeness. The other half of my hope lies in an indescribable, indefinable mystery that, thankfully, lies just beyond my grasp and my knowing, the pursuit of which gives my life meaning.

In the final analysis, writes Jung, our lives count for something only as we are related to that which is greater than we, by whatever image or name we choose to evoke and honor. If we are not related to such, our life is wasted. Evoking the image of *living spirit,* he concludes:

> The living spirit grows and even outgrows its earlier forms of expression. ... This living spirit is eternally renewed and pursues its goal in manifold and inconceivable ways throughout the history of mankind. Measured against it, the names and forms which men have given it mean very little; they are only the changing leaves and blossoms on the stem of the eternal tree (Jung 1958:538).

CHAPTER ONE

SPEAKING TO THE POLITICAL ELEPHANT IN THE ROOM

What we choose to fight is so tiny!
What fights us is so great!
When we win, it's with small things,
And the triumph makes us small.
This is how we grow:
by being defeated, decisively
by constantly greater mysteries.
(Wright, inspired by poems from Rilke's *Book of Hours*)

To employ ancient mystical language, I believe our nation and world are in a *collective dark night of the soul.* The darkness has thickened since the 2024 United States presidential election. Our collective souls are suffering, and our concerns are mounting. To address this critical time in our history, I want to draw on the language and insights of soul, on the modern science of soul, on psychology, and particularly on the Analytical Psychology of Carl Gustav Jung. For me, Jungian Psychology is the best language to navigate the darkness of the outer and inner landscape that we continue to learn is one.

The preceding paragraph was not my first choice for an opening essay for this third volume of the trilogy, nor my second nor third. I have lost count of the revisions.

The original title of this introductory essay was "The Trump Cult." For several weeks during the early part of Donald Trump's second presidency, I wrote furiously about the dangerous parallels between Trump and other historical cult figures and their followers. Cults form around authoritarian leaders who rule with an iron fist, who garner power for self-interests and narcissistic needs, who promise physical and monetary safety at any costs, and who show little concern for anyone outside the cult. Cult leaders have little or no capacity for empathy. They demand absolute loyalty, and dissenters risk being expelled or replaced.

I was, and remain, especially alarmed about the *religious* nature of the Trump Cult that assumes divine authority, validation, and power. Donald Trump hijacked large swaths of Christian evangelicals by pretending to be interested in religion. His public display of holding a Bible in front of a Washington, D.C., cathedral, and his antic of publishing and selling his own version of the Bible were laughable, except to those who fell for the carnival trick.

Of course, the cult leader had no interest in religion (evangelical or otherwise) except for the votes of religious and political conservatives. In return, he promised to support their conservative social agendas. Although he and many of his followers claimed Christian validation, I noted the erosion of the root values of honesty, kindness, civility, justice, and democracy, and the dismantling of humane institutions committed to compassion for the least among us. I also suggested that the massive deportations and incarcerations of immigrants, as well as the marginalization of individuals and groups who didn't fit with an exclusive, narrowly defined "American," were instances of the projection of the individual and collective shadow.

Many of the Trump administration's actions were accompanied with "God Bless America" and "In God We Trust." Those familiar phrases too often mean, "Our God is number one, and so are we! Because our country was founded on God, and by God, we are the favored nation, and BY GOD we plan to keep it that way!" The Trump religious cult is reminiscent of other times in our history when politics and religion were wed and permitted any and all heinous acts in the name of God. This current religious pathology is the latest outbreak of Monotheistic Madness that was identified in Volume One of this trilogy (Wright 2018:39ff).

As a Jungian psychoanalyst, my unofficial diagnosis that Donald J. Trump suffers from a narcissistic personality disorder seemed accurate. Among psychological professionals, the code of conduct advises against assigning a psychological diagnosis except in a structured clinical setting and relationship. However, President Trump exhibits his personality structure so freely, even proudly, that he invites diagnostic critique. For him it seems a badge of honor—the more scrutiny he receives, the more freedom he takes to exceed all boundaries.

As I made my case for the Trump Cult, I noted the dynamics of what Carl Jung identified as mob psychology that renders void rational thought and behavior by members of the mob or cult. Jung notes that the level of group consciousness is reduced to the lowest level of the leader and its least conscious members. For all his bravado, Donald Trump exhibits a very low, primitive level of consciousness. His lust for power is rooted in deep feelings of inferiority. He craves constant and universal adulation, alongside his constant self-aggrandizement. He suffers from a particular kind of disorder that causes him to believe his own lies, a condition shared by other dangerous leaders in history (Jung 1964:419). He has little awareness of, or concern for, the effects of his words and behavior on others. He is incapable of empathy.

As I looked over my writing shoulder, I referred to an essay that I wrote during Trump's first term. It described how members of a dysfunctional family rally around an abusive parent. They become identified with the abuser in an attempt to remain safe. Their fears override all other concerns, rationality, or values. This dynamic helps me understand why so many of our citizens, and especially political leaders, remain loyal to Donald Trump (Wright 2022:69-70). In the language of addiction and recovery, Donald Trump is addicted to power, and those who support him, no matter what he says or does, are codependent enablers. For the most part, Trump loyalists are unwitting enablers. They are reacting out of fear of a changing world and nostalgia for a past that no longer exists and was likely never as good as remembered. The promises of America being great again provide momentary relief from individual and collective fears—fears of change, fears of uncertainty, and fears of an unknown future.

Jungian Analyst and prolific author James Hollis reminds us that fear is a natural human response, but lives governed by fear can bring about devastating consequences. He writes, "We can now see how the Third Reich emerged in Germany, not as a one-time event but as something even stable societies suffer when difficult social situations weaken the ego's sense of management and bring about both depression and heightened anxiety" (Hollis 2025: xvii,118).

Finally, drawing on my two previous books that call for new images of God and religions that are more life-giving, I wrote voluminous pages on the emergence of authoritarian leaders and regimes that represent a regressive return to the patriarchy of supernatural monotheism. I noted the dangers and the similarities between the worst qualities of the patriarchal Father-God image, the Hollywood Godfather, and political leaders like Donald Trump who present and promote a powerful Father-God persona.

The current evangelical and political regression seems like a desperate attempt to preserve patriarchal religion and culture. Old fearful white men are afraid of losing their power and privileges, supposedly gifted to them by a white theistic Father-God. Religion is powerful because it links one with the supposed power attributed to the gods. Unconscious religion is deadly (Wright 2021:36).

Again, through numerous revisions of "The Trump Cult," I felt energized, even brilliant! I was on a writing roll! I imagined it would be a powerful and popular essay, especially for my like-minded, liberal friends and colleagues. Regardless of how it might be received, and because of the collective dis-ease in our nation and world, I knew I had to begin this volume by *speaking to the political elephant in the room.* Furthermore, it was a necessary and helpful outlet for some of my anger as part of election grief.

One morning after a night of disturbing dreams, I awoke with the question, *Will your essay provide more light on our dangerous divisions, or simply provide more heat?* Of course, I immediately knew the answer. Reluctantly, I let go of my attachment to my brilliant essay, while continuing to own that it had some validity.

I had to admit that my own political party had been guilty of dangerous, even deadly, policies such as continuing to be the arms dealer of the world while touting concerns for gun control at home. Or, pretending not to be at war while supplying our allies with billions of dollars worth of armaments. Or, deploring the barbaric acts of war crimes, such as beheadings, while supplying drones that blow people to bits. I had to admit that both political parties and their loyal followers, that is, each and all of us, are responsible for the darkness that surrounds us. I had to admit that it is easier to contribute to the dysfunction of politics than to the noble art of governing.

In retrospect, several doubts had begun to creep into the edges of my consciousness even as I was making a legitimate case for a Trump Cult. While nearly half of our citizens were depressed and enraged over the election results, a little more than half were ecstatic. Furthermore, if the results had been reversed, so would the mourners and celebrants. How could political preferences be a simple issue of right or wrong when the 2024 election reversed the previous one, and a future one may well be another reversal?

Had Kamala Harris and the Democrats won the election, there would have been an equal outcry, perhaps cast as another stolen election as was the case during the previous four years. In any case, a similar level of passion and perceived "rightness" would be present. We would still be talking about how divided we are and how the gap continues to widen between left and right, blue and red states, the haves and the have nots, gay and straight, east and west, and numerous other perceived differences. And our individual and collective fears, even terrors, would continue to mount. To conclude that millions of voters, Democratic or Republican, were simply wrong or deluded was not satisfying. Something was not right with this picture as I struggled to make sense, and meaning, of the surrounding darkness.

Eventually, laying aside my political lens, including my personal political preferences, I retrieved my depth psychological lens to try to sort out what might be beneath our perceived differences and our genuine fears. That is when I crafted the opening paragraph.

With fresh eyes, a psychological eyeglass, and the language of soul, I took another look at the collective darkness that seemed so frightening. I realized afresh that our fears are not that we are so divided, and so far apart. Rather, it is because we are so close! We are so frightened because, in the faces of the others, we are often looking at ourselves in a mirror—up close and personal. In the faces of those across the political aisle or across the street, of those who have different cultural, religious, or sexual values, of those who are perceived as opponents or enemies, we are seeing our unconscious *shadow selves*. We are seeing aspects of ourselves that we would rather not see.

It is ironic that we are closer to each other than ever because of our amazing communication technologies, and, at the same time, we are more afraid of each other. Even though we are so close, our eyes are clouded with suspicion and paranoia. The daily, moment by moment mirrors of others provide a glimpse of our shadow selves.

This is the language and light of depth psychology. We come face to face with aspects of ourselves that we have forgotten, repressed, supposedly eliminated, or at least kept hidden. We see aspects of ourselves that we are ashamed of, or that frighten us. We come face to face with images of ourselves that are the opposite of our carefully crafted self-images.

Again, through the lens of depth psychology, our fears are not rooted in how different we are, or how far apart we are, but how very close we are, how very similar. We now know this fact cosmologically, biologically, and psychologically. A very thin space separates us from everyone and everything else. That small space is the battleground for all of our political disagreements, divisions, and wars. That highly charged space is also where love and intimacy happen. Of course, that space can also be frightening because we are so close, so vulnerable.

To say it succinctly, the small space between us and the other gets filled with all manner of *projected* material. The dynamics of *psychological projection* are generally misunderstood or ignored even though they are active in all relationships. Those issues and relationships that evoke intense emotion—like our current politics—alert us to aspects of our unconscious that desire to come into the light of consciousness. The greater the intensity, the more likely a projective process is at work. Volume One includes a thorough review of the subject under the title "Projection and Revelation." Contrary to the popular view that projection is pathological and needs to be avoided, projection is *natural, necessary, and purposeful.* Its purpose is to reveal (Wright 2018:83ff). In the context of this essay, its purpose would be to reveal light for our *collective dark night of the soul.*

Psychological projection is initiated by the autonomy of the deep unconscious. This perspective stands in sharp contrast to the popular, shallow notion that projection is a voluntary function of the ego, as "you should not project your shadow onto others" or "he projected his anima onto that beautiful woman." Projections are initiated by the unconscious itself, by that inner/invisible mystery that I prefer to call the Wisdom of the psyche or soul. This distinction grants psychological projection its autonomy, its power, and its mystical, revelatory purpose.

Throughout his *Collected Works*, Jung seemed never to tire of underscoring this vital distinction. Writing about the origin of projections, Jung says "it is not the conscious subject but the unconscious which does the projecting. Hence one meets with projections, one does not make them" (Jung 1948:17). As if addressing the metaphor of this essay, the *collective dark night of the soul*, Jung writes, "Projection is never made; it happens, it is simply there. In the darkness of anything external to me I find, without recognizing it as such, an interior or psychic life that is my own" (Jung 1943a:346). Thus, the role of the ego is to recognize the projection, to withdraw it, and to own it as part of one's own interior life, one's own personality.

In its simplest description, psychological projection is a subtle process whereby contents of one's own unconscious are perceived to be outside oneself or in others. Jung reminds us that "it is a natural and given thing for unconscious contents to be projected … all the contents of our unconscious are constantly being projected into our surroundings, so much so that projections change the world into the replica of one's unknown face" (Jung 1959a:17). Furthermore, projection is so natural and fundamental that it has taken several thousand years of civilization to become aware of it (Jung 1943a:6). What we reject in ourselves "is apt to turn up in the guise of a hostile neighbor, who will inevitably arouse your anger and make you aggressive. It is surely better to know that your worst enemy is right there in your own heart" (Jung 1964b:456). Or in the words of Friedrich Nietzsche, "He who fights with monsters might take care lest he thereby become a monster" (Wright 2018:95).

With his combination of mystical heart and psychological mind, Thomas Merton declared that all wars begin with the human heart/psyche and are fueled by our individual refusal to deal with our private, internal wars, our conflicted selves. From this perspective, our best efforts at peacemaking will be to deal with our shadow, our personal little wars. Our internal civil wars may well determine whether our species thrives or dies.

Circling back to the theme of this essay, for a crash course on psychological projection, we only have to watch and listen to our political leaders, *or pay close attention to our own arguments.* With rare exceptions, what is uttered or publicized about an opponent is a mirror of unconscious contents of the speaker. One might say a "naked mirror" because one is exposing oneself, at least to the psychological eye. The heated debates around passionate issues—gun control, abortion, sexuality, national security, immigration, religion—are generally devoid of basic psychological insight or wisdom. The problem is always in the other person or party. As I explore in another essay, scapegoating is a way to hide from one's own shadow. Knowing the subtle ways the shadow operates has made it very difficult to craft this essay. I do not claim exemption from psychological projection!

With outer others who arouse intense emotions within us, we discover aspects of our hidden selves that desire to come into consciousness. The intense emotion can range from fear and repulsion to attraction and desire. In the former, our so-called *dark shadow* is being aroused. In the latter, it is our *bright shadow.* As Jungian analyst Robert Johnson was fond of reminding us, both are considered to be *inner gold* because both add to the wholeness of our personality.

James Hollis describes the shadow as whatever is within us we wish not to face. He writes:

> If we wish to learn more about the shadow, we must look to our history, but more to our fears. Where the fears are is the shadow's dwelling, and it renews its course in our life through sundry disguises as projection onto others, repression of a vital part of ourselves, or as a narrowing of life—the wearing of shoes too small (Hollis 2003:47).

In his book *On This Journey We Call Our Lives,* Hollis reminds us that the shadow "embodies the contrarian dimensions of our souls. Put most succinctly, what is wrong in the world is in us as well. As the Latin playwright Terence wrote over two millennia ago, *Nothing human is alien to me.* So, the work of improving the world begins in my own backyard" (Hollis 2020:126-27). Hollis then turns to Jung for a definitive description of one who takes on the shadow. Such a person, writes Jung,

> ... has become a serious problem to himself, as he is now unable to say *they* do this or that, *they* are wrong, and *they* must be fought against ... Such a man knows that whatever is wrong in the world is in himself, and if he only learns to deal with his own shadow he has done something real for the world. He has succeeded in shouldering an infinitesimal part of the gigantic, unsolved social problems of our day (Jung 1958c:140).

With consciousness of our own shadow, and our capacity for psychological projection on any topic, at any moment, we may still need to address obvious violations of justice, fairness, and equality perpetuated by other individuals or groups. As we do so, however, a sign that our legitimate critique has activated our own shadow may be the *delight* we feel when our opponent fails or is caught in shady activities. The German word for this is *schadenfreude.* Websites, podcasts, and cable news channels devoted solely to demeaning and mocking political opponents simply add to our collective darkness. To use a previous metaphor, they promote more heat than light. They can be a convenient hiding place for the individual and the collective shadow.

Finally, the human shadow loves jokes and humor. When we laugh at a joke, it is our shadow that has caught the absurdity, the paradox, the surprise turn. People who are humorless or who cannot take an affectionate joke or ribbing are generally out of touch with their darker shadow—and they are not very good company. On the other hand, the use of humor can also be a hiding place for the dark shadow, and this is especially true for political humor during these intense politically divisive days. There is a fine line between being funny and being demeaning and cruel. There is something within us that knows where that line is and when it has been crossed. Good humor is an art form, and we need more of it in these dark days. Humor that has a hidden axe to grind feels just like that.

During our *collective dark night of the soul*, I am grateful that many people of different political stripes work daily to make our nation and world a more hospitable habitat. Some do this in visible, public ways, while others go unnoticed. Many, however, feel paralyzed to know what to do to make a difference because the issues seem so complicated and the darkness so deep. Consulting the dynamics of the psychology of soul—recognizing, withdrawing, and owning our own dark shadow—may be the best gift we can offer others. Owning our own shadow will require no executive action, no congressional approval, no appropriation of large sums of money. It will require careful attention to the moment-by-moment relational exchange in that sacred space between us and all others.

CHAPTER TWO

THE GODS WE BIRTH

What are we humans, after all
but gods in the making,
and making the wrong god makes
the wrong kind of world in which to live.
(Ilia Delio)

Dear ones, beware,
beware of the tiny gods frightened men worship
to bring an anesthetic control and relief
to their sad days.
(Hafiz)

Our species has been birthing images of gods and religious ideas since the dawn of reflective consciousness. The evolutionary gift and burden of human consciousness appeared in the most recent 200,000 years, a mere blink of cosmological time. Our ancestors found themselves in a mysterious world and were compelled to begin asking the existential questions that continue to this very moment: Who am I? Why am I here? And collectively, where did we come from, and where do we go when we die? Speaking more poetically, what is the meaning of this brief sojourn between the birth I did not request and the death I cannot escape?

In their instinctual search for meaning (what Carl Jung calls the religious instinct), our ancestors began to tell stories about their experiences of the numinous visible world, as well as their felt experiences of powers and presences just beyond sight, yet nevertheless real. With their imagination, along with what we now know as *psychological projection*, their world was quickly populated with invisible powers and presences that they named gods, goddesses, and spirits, and each was assigned a name and a role to play in the visible and invisible domains. Numinous experiences were shared and elaborated, and larger stories called myths, religions, and religious rituals were born.

Archaeological and cultural artifacts reveal that all tribes and cultures had some form of acknowledgement of an invisible world alongside, beneath, or beyond the visible domain. Forces that governed that mysterious reality ranged from theistic gods and goddesses to universal energies like Tao, Brahman, Great Spirit, Mind, and Self. In the case of theistic gods and goddesses, most divinities served a particular purpose, enjoyed a limited lifespan, and were replaced by the imaginations of subsequent generations and cultures. Again, each and all were birthed through the human psyche and imagination, necessarily so, as is all human knowledge.

The human psyche is the *organic gateway* through which all psychological life and knowledge enters, and through which our particular life finds expression. Jung reminds us that without the psyche there would be neither knowledge nor insight. The human psyche is the experiencer, the interpreter, the recorder, the decider, and the actor of all that happens. While this is an obvious fact, too often we have imagined the human soul/psyche as nothing more than an object to be saved for an afterlife.

In other words, all of our experiences are first of all psychological. Once we begin to name, interpret, and express an experience, it takes on other designations or names. This is why I propose that psychology precedes theology, and any other discipline or "ology." Throughout these pages, I have chosen to use the verb *birth* rather than *create*. Birth is more psychologically accurate to honor the ego's dependence on the collective or archetypal unconscious, the metaphorical storehouse of images that seek out consciousness. The human ego is more of a midwife than a creator. For these reasons, I have chosen to employ *birth*.

The birth of a one-and-only supreme deity, God, is a rather recent addition to the cosmic scene and drama. Generally considered to be a transcendent, supernatural male being, he was birthed by the human psyche and imagination approximately 4,000 years ago. He was soon considered to be a lot older. To stave off competition from other divinities, this particular God-image was granted eternal status, before the beginning of time and beyond time and beyond space. He was "grandfathered in" and retains a grandfather persona for many. He was also claimed to be the *only* God; thus, the idea of monotheism entered the religious lexicon.

The monotheistic God of Abraham remains loosely shared by Judaism, Christianity, and Islam. Monotheism has attracted millions of devoted followers over the centuries. It has also promoted perpetual militaristic competition, conflict, war, and bloodshed. The initial battleground was a small tract of Middle East desert that came to be called Holy. The battlefield gradually spread around the globe as religion and politics were wed. Battles continue to this day over which religious tribe God favors. The so-called Holy Land remains a battleground for repeated outbreaks of Monotheistic Madness identified in Volume One (Wright 2018:39ff). The war in Gaza between Hamas and Israel, with the support of numerous allies on both sides, including the United States, is one of the latest outbreaks of religious *madness.*

Volume One, *Reimagining God and Religion*, also proposed that the lifespan of the monotheistic myth and its image of a Father-God has ended. To use the vernacular, the expiration dates for the monotheistic myth and its core god-image have passed, along with the image of a three-tiered universe. Dangerously dualistic from its inception, the monotheistic God-image and its myth, as necessary as they were once upon a time, are out of date, yet not out of mind (Wright 2018:32ff).

Even though the god-image has expired, Father-God continues to rule the *unconscious* of much of the religious world. Furthermore, the influence of the powerful image has not been restricted to religions. It continues to shape other aspects of human life, including cultural attitudes of the superiority of men over women and masculine values over feminine values. As noted in the previous essay, the patriarchal aspect of God the Father is currently manifesting in the *cultish*, power politics of the United States, as well as of many other nations.

Meanwhile, from the perspective of Jung's Analytical Psychology, a new religious myth is seeking consciousness from the mysterious depths of the unconscious from whence all psychological life emerges. Jung's comment on a dream of psychoanalyst Max Zeller suggests that a new collective myth is being birthed, yet it will likely have a long gestation period. Jung also noted that foundations for the new myth are already in place and many people are dedicated to its birth. (For the dream of Max Zeller and Jung's commentary, see pages 79-80 in Volume One, *Reimagining God and Religion*.)

It has been proposed that Analytical Psychology was birthed to fill the religious void created by the decline, demise, and metaphorical death of theism and monotheism. In this interim time between religious myths that are no longer viable and new ones yet to be birthed, the insights of depth psychology are especially timely and helpful. Speaking to the theme of this brief essay, Jungian psychology provides a reliable picture of how gods, goddesses, and God came to be in the first place.

God-images and religions are birthed by the human imagination. They are inspired by numinous experiences that we do not create, cannot control, and cannot command to appear. Once primary experiences of the sacred are shared, dogmatized, and canonized, they die. Their death, however, may be denied for years, even for generations, as is the case today. It seems easier to nod to the religions of our ancestors than to respond to our own experiences of the numinous, a word that means *a nod from the gods* (Wright 2021:70).

From the perspective of the dynamics of *psychological projection,* our images of gods, goddesses, and God are unconscious aspects of ourselves seen in projected forms. Our gods are mirrors of our deepest desires, longings, instincts, hopes, dreams, and fears that we see via psychological projection. They are mirrors that reflect back to us latent capacities of creativity and destruction that we share with Nature itself. Our gods are our best and worst instincts seen in projection. The god-images we have birthed are the mirrors we hold up before ourselves, reflections by which we apprehend and comprehend our own being. They reveal nothing of literal external entities, yet they reveal to us our most important values and latent capacities for great creativity and great destruction, our capacities for great good and great evil. The acceptance of the human potential for creativity and destruction, for extraordinary acts of sacrificial love and of unspeakable evil avoids the psychological either/or splitting that has characterized the one-sided monotheistic myth.

Again, in many respects we have to see aspects of ourselves in projected forms before we can recognize them as our own. Psychologically, we birth our gods in an effort to understand ourselves and our place and purpose in the mysterious universe.

To recall the essay "Speaking to the Political Elephant in the Room," we often see unconscious aspects of ourselves on the faces of those we idealize and/or demonize. Psychological projection works rather continuously to aid our self-knowledge. When we imagine divine beings, the same projective dynamics enable us to recognize our unconscious godlike capacities for creativity and destruction. Psychological projection validates those mystical traditions that speak of "the god who dwells within you as you."

Of course, there is great hesitation to abandon the image of God as an external, supernatural, interventionist Being. The hesitation often centers around the fear that there would be no ultimate values, no order, no ethics, and the world would be a chaotic free-for-all. The expressed fear is that with no God in heaven we could do as we please without restraint here on Earth. Actually, when god-images are internalized as capacities of our own psyche/soul, we are compelled to a higher ethic, rather than a lesser one. We bear more responsibility, not less.

Personally, I am no longer concerned about a supposed external, supernatural, interventionist deity, or external saviors, or Armageddon endings. I am more concerned about the deity-like and devil-like capacities we humans possess and the lack of consciousness of that psychological fact. I am more concerned about the low level of consciousness of those who make our laws, who guard our nuclear weapons, and who insist that they have been chosen by the one-and-only God to do so.

Stated another way, we must stop spending so much of our time and energy trying to discern the character, will, and purpose of supposed external deities, and devote that same energy to understanding the human psyche. We must stop praying to external deities to help us clean up the messes of our own making, and we must cease preying on each other and our fragile, limited Earth. This is the great turning that must happen, that will happen, as our religious consciousness expands and deepens.

Near the end of his long career, Carl Jung warned that our future hangs by a very thin thread, and that thread, he proposed, is the human psyche about which we know very little. In these sobering times, the thread that holds us feels very fragile. Jung's prophetic words are as fresh as the morning news:

> It is my conviction that the investigation of the psyche is the science of the future ... it is becoming ever more obvious that it is not famine, not earthquakes, nor microbes, not cancer but man himself who is man's greatest danger to man, for the simple reason that there is no adequate protection against psychic epidemics, which are infinitely more devastating than the worst of natural disasters. The supreme danger which threatens individuals as well as whole nations is a *psychic danger.* The greatest danger of all comes from the masses in whom the effects of the unconscious pile up cumulatively and the reasonableness of the conscious mind is

> stifled. Every mass organization is a latent danger just as much as a heap of dynamite is ... Not by arming to the teeth, each for itself, can the nations defend themselves in the long run from the frightful catastrophes of modern war. The heaping up of arms is itself a call to war. Rather must they recognize those psychic conditions under which the unconscious bursts the dykes of consciousness and overwhelms it (Jung 1958:1358).

The old, external, supernatural gods that we have imagined, named, and have kept at a safe distance can no longer help us. We must bring them home to the human psyche, where they originated and where they belong. They have been orphaned too long. As radical and insensitive as it may sound, we must say goodbye to "Our Father in Heaven" and assume our parental responsibilities. We "Children of God" must grow up.

CHAPTER THREE

PSYCHOLOGICAL MYSTICISM

Go to the limits of your longing,
flare up like a flame
and make big shadows the gods can play in.
Let everything happen to you: beauty and terror.
Just keep going. No feeling is final.
(Wright, inspired by poems from Rilke's *Book of Hours*)

We are living in difficult times. Strange times. Scary times. Uncertain times. There are many responses to our collective predicament. Some are tempted to return to an idealized former time, to the good old days that seem safer, more secure. The United States and other nations are responding by electing authoritarian leaders who promise to rule with power. Some of us are striking out in rage and violence. Many others have given up trying to make meaning and are simply trying to make it through the day by medicating overwhelming misery or by engaging in the large supply of modern distractions.

Psychologically and spiritually, we are between collective stories, between myths—between a myth that provided some sense of our place and role in the universe while waiting for a new myth to appear. While we wait, some of us find meaning by actively imagining the outlines of a new myth. It is helpful to think of ourselves as midwives, assisting the birth of a larger wisdom that seeks out our consciousness. That is my desire, my hope, my reason for writing.

As I have wondered about, worried about, written and spoken about our current predicament and our future, the name of a possible new psychospiritual paradigm has presented itself—*Psychological Mysticism.* Borrowing lovely words from my friend and former Poet Laureate of North Carolina Cathy Smith Bowers, the phrase has become an *abiding image* and a *guiding metaphor.*

This chapter will circumambulate the abiding image to consider its potential width and depth as a bridge paradigm while we await the more fully developed collective myth. Drawing entries from my daily journal, as well as selected entries from the first two volumes of this trilogy, my intent is to describe psychological mysticism, rather than to define it. As always, readers are invited to read with journal in hand to attend the images and meanings that rise up from within. Again, this is what I mean by *magnetic reading* or *deep reading.*

At midlife, I left the familiarity and safety of the Church and moved to its metaphorical back porch. There I stayed for a while until the foundations of the theological porch collapsed as well, thrusting me out into the unknown as a wandering pilgrim. Chapters one and two of *Reimagining God and Religion* chronicle that difficult, and necessary, transition.

Among the many gifts of that transition has been the release of my religious imagination from its collective Christian imprisonment. Historically, that incarceration happened over its first few centuries as the Church took on the persona of a religious institution. Slowly abandoning its primary mission as care of the human soul and the soul of the natural world in favor of institutional maintenance, the Church also lost its imagination. This loss was solidified by dogma, creeds, and the closing of the scriptural canon in the third century. The closing of the canon was tantamount to severing its link to continuing revelation and transformation.

In the second half of my life, the release of my religious imagination has taken me into my professional passions—Jungian Psychology, Celtic Spirituality, and the mystical aspects of religion. In my search for a replacement for the monotheistic myth and God-image, which I left in the chancel and creeds of the Church, I discovered psychological mysticism. I don't remember coming across this phrase in my reading and research over the years. If so, I do not mean to steal it without due credit. It seemed to appear one day from that mystical storehouse called the collective unconscious. It continues to fertilize my imagination. It is sufficiently deep enough and wide enough to hold multiple meanings, as well as multiple religious/spiritual orientations. The paradigm can also be embraced by those who have no interest in identifying with religion or spirituality, yet who value living with consciousness and compassion.

While Jungian Psychology may be the most adequate current discipline for the integration of psychology and religion, it will need to continue to transform. Like all living entities, including religions and religious myths, Jungian Psychology will be replaced by a discipline even more relevant and life-giving.

As I live into the image, psychological mysticism is addressed to those who have left (or who would like to leave) the confines of a religious myth wed to an outdated, patriarchal, dualistic worldview; those who have grown weary of monotheistic religions that promote division, exclusivity, and malignant tribalism; and those who find other religions equally valid in approaching the Sacred Source or Ultimate Reality.

Psychological mysticism is for those who value the human mind and the discoveries of modern science, including depth psychology, as avenues of continuing revelation. The paradigm is meant for those who have a felt-sense that the divine encounter happens within and spreads outward, rather than coming from a remote, external, metaphysical deity. It will likely speak to those who hunger and thirst for the experience of the numinous, which has unlimited manifestations and innumerable names, and to which all can bow and none can control or possess. Psychological mysticism cuts through centuries of dogmatic theology and speculation about external supernatural deities and devils. The mystical perspective is one of radical immanence.

Rooted in Jungian Psychology, psychological mysticism does something that theology and most theologians rarely do: It makes the vital distinction between *god* and *god-image*. In his dialogues with the theologians of his day, Jung consistently made this distinction. He later acknowledged that he wished he had made that distinction in all his writings. From Jung's perspective, all our words and names for gods, goddesses, and God are *god-images*; that is, they are metaphors for a mystery that is ultimately unknown and unnamable. In a letter in 1957, Jung writes, "One must always remember that God is a mystery, and everything we say about it is said and believed by humans. We make images and concepts, and when I speak of God I always mean the image man has made of him" (Jung 1957: p. 384). Commenting further on Jung's words, James Hollis writes, "Put another way, it is humans, not gods, who make theology, and their constructs reveal more about them than about the inexplicable mystery ..." (Hollis 2025:115).

James Hollis has written the seminal book on the distinction between god and god-image. In *Tracking the Gods: The Place of Myth in Modern Life,* he says, "... the gods are the dynamic energies that rise out of archetypal encounters. They leave their traces in luminous images, but the images are not the gods; they are the temporary containers of that divine energy" (Hollis 1995:116). Again, "The image is not the god, but the image is so affectively charged as to reconnect us to the depth experience. What the ultimate mysteries are, of course, we cannot say" (Ibid, p. 103).

For most theologians and religious folk, in Jung's day as well as now, the name "God" is the mystery itself. In its popular usage, God is considered to be a noun, usually a supernatural Being. Psychologically, the name *god* is an image, a metaphor for mysteries that are beyond human comprehension. The distinction between *god* and *god-image* remains one of Jungian Psychology's most important contributions to religion and spirituality.

Theology begins with the assumption of an eternal, supernatural, divine Being. Psychology begins with human experiences, some of which are designated divine. Here the waters of knowledge divide. I have been swimming in both streams for most of my adult life. The streams have converged, and now I am walking a path I call psychological mysticism. Walking this path requires no less trust in the mysterious currents of life in its purposeful unfolding, yet requires far more responsibility for our human choices and behavior. Old cliches like "leave it up to God" or "the Devil made me do it" are no longer viable.

Psychological mysticism differs from theological mysticism in many respects. Generally speaking, theological mysticism, and theology in general, focus on *transcendence*, on connecting or reconnecting with that which transcends matter and ordinary human life. Emphasis is placed on transcending one's self, one's human desires by connecting with that which is above, beyond, or outside physical life. Theological mystical experiences are considered to be otherworldly and usually limited to a few special people or saints.

On the other hand, psychological mysticism focuses the imagination on *descendance*, on immanence, on radical immanence, on unconscious depths— thus, depth psychology. It humanizes and equalizes the mystical experience, recognizing that the mystical sense is our species' sixth sense. The mystical sense is a human inheritance, part of our innate wiring. We differ only in the attention to its recognition and development.

We are born mystics
married to mystery
tethered to the unbreakable sacred umbilical
divorce not possible
destined to be and to become

the conscious deities and devils
long seen in projected guise.
(Wright 2021:46-47)

Analytical Psychology was birthed, I think, to help us recover our connection to, and relationship with, the invisible aspect of Ultimate Reality, and to deepen our relationships with the visible aspect. Jung's psychology provides both a language and disciplines to honor life in its visible and invisible wholeness.

When we are most alive and vital, we live on the threshold between the visible and invisible, and we move back and forth as necessary. Each night we receive glimpses of what is on the other side of the veil between the two. During the day, as well, the invisible manifests in the events and relationships that we experience. Psychological mysticism teaches us how to pay attention to the outside and inside, the above and beneath, the visible and invisible, and the beautiful and ugly of all that we encounter. Such careful, responsive attention constitutes a psychological mystical attitude toward life.

I share Jung's chief concern that we no longer have a living myth that honors the invisible world and the necessity of our ongoing relationship with it. We have assigned the invisible half of Reality to external deities, devils, and angels while we content our suffering selves with that which is visible and rational.

When a culture no longer has a life-giving myth, any number of ideologies fill the void. Jung once noted that many of those pseudo-myths end with an "ism," as in rationalism, literalism, fundamentalism, materialism, voyeurism, nationalism, and consumerism. Currently, the so-called developed nations of the world, including the United States, seem to trust a myth of "More and More. Bigger and Better." If the unconscious, unspoken myth was verbalized, it would sound something like: *Do not worry. Something or someone will save us if only we keep consuming more and more!*

Surely more is always better
Along with bigger and higher
And being great again.

How dare that Jewish rabbi
Propose otherwise
That less is more
The first shall be last
And vice versa
That the greatest are servants of all?

What was that homeless
Itinerant mystic smoking
Declaring happy are the humble
And the peacemakers and the poor in spirit?

What did he know
He who had only twelve followers
On his Twitter account?
(Wright 2021:107-08)

Rooted in depth psychology, psychological mysticism addresses the concerns of that ancient, yet ever-new, word "soul." Psyche is the Greek word for soul and reminds us that we are, finally, the animal that desires meaning and suffers its loss (Hollis 2020:23). James Hollis reminds us that we can neither purchase meaning nor create it. He writes:

> Meaning is a by-product of being in right relationship to our souls at critical junctions. If what we are doing is right for us, no matter how perilous the path, we are supported from within; our suffering, our investment, our uncertainty are rewarded with purposefulness. This cannot be faked, and over time, even the most troubled of journeys seem rich with meaning (Ibid., p.108).

A mystical consciousness includes the moment-by-moment awareness of the parallel processes between the visible and invisible aspects of the one Reality. Whatever is happening in the outer, visible world has its corresponding inner, invisible process or meaning. Ancient wisdom expressed these parallel processes with phrases like *As Above, So Below* or *As Outer, So Inner.* Depth psychology employs the language of *conscious* and *unconscious* to speak of similar phenomena.

From the perspective of psychological mysticism, the visible/invisible, outer/inner, matter/spirit aspects of life are two sides of the same religious coin. They are of equal value. Balance and mutuality are the optimal goals; imbalance brings about distress and dis-ease. Jung described the mutuality of matter and spirit by saying *matter is the visible aspect of spirit* and *spirit is the invisible aspect of matter.* This psychological slant is a necessary correction to the dualistic monotheistic myth that elevates the spiritual world over the material world, and its accompanying denigration of the body and sexuality.

The foundations of psychological mysticism are experiences of the *numinous,* a word coined by Rudolph Otto and borrowed by Jung for the cornerstone of his psychology.

Such experiences:

- Are universal, common to all regardless of culture or religious identity or lack thereof;
- Appear unbidden, called or not called, invited or not;
- Do not require belief in an external, supernatural, interventionist deity or deities;
- Do not require a supernatural savior, messiah, or mediator;
- Do not require a human mediator, or an infallible sacred text;
- Register first in the body, validating the body as a sacred vessel;
- Are multivalent, nondual, include ecstasy and terror, delight and dread, light and dark, and what we experience as both good and evil. (Wright 2021:83ff).

Numinous moments are human universals, experienced as a spontaneous presence or power. They come unbidden. They wash upon our souls' shores, continuously lapping at us wavelike, sometimes gently and at other times with hurricane or tsunami force. They do not respect geographical bounaries or ask for a religious ID or require adherence to dogmaţic beliefs. As such, the experiences of the numinous provide a sacred path beyond tribal religions that threaten our species and planet.

Attending numinous experiences and seeking to serve as a conscious conduit for them constitutes a religious attitude from the perspective of Jungian Psychology and psychological mysticism. Living with such an attitude fuels the process of individuation by which one grows in intimate relationship with unconscious contents and empathic, compassionate connection to all.

Numinous…
A Mystical nod from the gods
Coined by Otto, borrowed by Jung.
When the gods come a-nodding
On the mystical path less traveled
A humble bow
Or seventy times seven
Will suffice
To mark all places and all times as holy.
(Wright 2021:83-85)

Speaking about the experience of the numinous, Jung writes that the *numinosum* is "an invisible presence that causes a peculiar alteration in consciousness" (Jung 1958c:6). In his 2024 book titled *Awe*, Dacher Keltner comes to a similar conclusion in his vast research of the experience of wonder and awe, which are the emotions that often accompany a numinous encounter. The subtitle of his book is "The New Science of Everyday Wonder and How It Can Transform Your Life." Keltner asked a vast number of subjects in a wide variety of circumstances, "When have you encountered a vast mystery that transcends your understanding of the world?" (Keltner 2024:1-20) His fascinating book documents the power of awe to transform one's consciousness.

In a letter to P. W. Martin in August 1945, Carl Jung wrote, "You are quite right, the main interest in my work is not concerned with the treatment of neurosis but rather with the approach to the *numinous*. But the fact is that the approach to the numinous is the real therapy and inasmuch as you attain to the numinous experiences you are released from the curse of pathology" (Jung 1945b:376-77).

Again, the psychological mystical path is a natural, inclusive, and potentially soul-satisfying path for the modern person. It does not require belief in a supernatural theistic being that is separate from the natural world. It requires no complicated religious dogma or adherence to a set of beliefs or sacred texts that were authoritative for our ancestors. Psychological mysticism does not require the mediation of sacred experience by another person, priest, or religious authority.

The primary invitation is to pay reverential attention to the mysteries that surround and infuse us moment by moment. We are continually approached by unconscious contents that we do not create or control, that we may or may not understand, and yet we feel compelled to respond. The unsolicited experiences may approach from the visible (so-called outer) or from the invisible (so-called inner) domain of the one Reality. They meet us in solitude or in community, and during the day or night.

Responses to the mysteries that surround and infuse us range from delight to dread, from awe to disinterest, from ecstasy to terror, from intense curiosity to apathy. We may feel compelled to move toward or to retreat. In Jung's psychological framework, to honor with reverential attention the unbidden mysteries that approach us constitutes a *religious attitude.* Such an attitude also describes a *psychological mystic.*

We are born mystics
Squeezed through the thin place
in the cosmic curtain
Suddenly a lifetime threshold-dweller
between visible and invisible
light and dark
Always on the edge
of the mystical path
Animated and enlivened.
(Wright 2021:46)

Carl Jung's extensive writings provide a unique witness to *psychological mysticism* as compared to *theological mysticism.* In the former, one encounters the divine essence in the depths of life and in the depths of the psyche. In the latter, the experience of the divine is perceived to emanate from the heavenly heights, from a divine being outside physical life. The invisible powers and presences that Jung personally encountered, and those reported by classic mystics like Meister Eckhardt, Jacob Boehme, and

Mechthild of Magdeburg, were considered to be *holy immanent* rather than *wholly transcendent.* Jung was keenly interested in their mystical experiences and writings. He saw their experiences as symbolic processes at work in the psychic depths, processes natural to all persons.

The psychological approach supports a grounded, embodied mysticism as compared to what is all too often a heavenly, disembodied escapism. The latter continues to plague monotheistic religions and their followers, regardless of efforts to spin the outdated worldview and myth. Psychological mysticism reverses what could be called "trickle-down theology and religion," whereby the resources of a remote divinity trickle down to Earth and humanity through a religious hierarchy. Just as trickle-down economics continues to fail, trickle-down religion can no longer be supported by modern consciousness. There is no hierarchy of divine life or divine favor. If there were, it would likely emanate from the bottom up, from the depths of life rather than from the heights. From the perspective of psychological mysticism, our salvation will not come from the heights of heaven or from a supernatural intervention or a promised messiah. If our species is to survive and thrive, it will demand that we embrace our collective godlike powers of creativity and destruction and incarnate them responsibly.

Psychological mysticism takes one deeper into life, into the natural world, rather than lifting one out of life and away from the Earth. It is a state of *descendance* as compared to *transcendence.* The goal is to be a full participant in ordinary, natural life rather than to achieve a supernatural existence, either before or after death.

Psychological mysticism promises meaningful participation in the mysteries of life rather than easy answers to life's puzzles.

The goal of following a mystical path is not happiness or a state of bliss. Contentment would be a more accurate designation. Contentment suggests the capacity to engage life as it is, in its inevitable mixture, without withdrawal into self-pity, bitterness, or resignation. Equally, it means to be free to celebrate life's joys, ecstasies, and windfalls without hesitation or neurotic guilt. Contentment avoids the state of psychological inflation that accompanies narcissism, and the state of psychological deflation that comes with victimhood. None of us is as good and holy as we imagine, nor as bad and unredeemable as we fear. Contentment allows us to pitch our tent at a psychological sea level.

Psychological mysticism suggests that we meet god disguised as our life, including all of life's mixtures and textures. It is a practical or pragmatic mysticism that embraces *what is*, and how we live *what is* responsibly. This validates Jung's response near the end of his life when he talked about his definition of God. His reply: "This is the name by which I designate all things which cross my wilful path violently and recklessly, all things which upset my subjective views, plans, and intentions and change the course of my life for better or worse" (Jung 1960: 525).

Likewise, in one of his last interviews Jung was asked if he believed in God. After a reflective pause, he replied, "I no longer believe. I know" (Jung 1977:428). His response could well be considered a mystical one, thus validating charges by orthodox theologians that he was a mystic. Their use of the term, however, was a way to dismiss his experiential approach to religious realities as illegitimate. Unfortunately, mystics and mysticism remain suspect in theological circles, or they are reserved for select individuals.

Personally, when I am asked what I mean when I use the word "gods," I often reply with some version of "I mean the mysterious animating energies, powers, and felt-presences at the heart of all matter, and at the heart of all that does matter." This satisfies my mind, my heart, and the mystic in me.

The primary concerns of psychological mysticism are *relationships*, rather than *redemption*. This includes relationship with our bodies and psychological depths, relationship with the mysterious Cosmos and Earth of which we are an organic part, and relationship with all others with whom we are intrinsically linked.

The focus on *relationships* replaces the focus on *redemption* and *atonement,* which have been primary concerns of Christian theology before and after the Reformation and Counter-Reformation. Matthew Fox notes that it was the redemption motif that fueled the religious invasions and destruction of indigenous peoples in Africa, in the Americas, and in the Pacific islands. Such barbarisms were given credence by three notorious papal bulls of the 15th century that were known as the "Doctrine of Discovery." Those unfortunate religious pronouncements essentially viewed people and lands as property to be brought into the Christian fold at whatever the costs, and the costs were tremendous. We continue to reap the horrible harvest of such "redemptive" efforts. I have referred elsewhere to such religious pathology as Monotheistic Madness.

The monotheistic myth and God-image continue to rule the unconscious of large segments of the world's population. When they were birthed by the human imagination approximately 4,000 years ago, they were consistent with the current knowledge of that day. They were also consistent with the level of collective consciousness of the day. We now know so much more about the visible-outer world and the invisible-psychological world. The level of human consciousness also continues to widen and deepen, albeit very slowly.

Monotheism suffers from what might be called a "double dualism." First, it imagines a God prior to and separate from the created order. This dualism has given rise to the divisions between heaven/earth, spiritual/physical, and spirit/matter. Second, the monotheistic myth imagines the human species to be elevated above the natural world, with the added command to "subdue" it. This dualism has given rise to our treatment of nature as an object to use and consume. Unfortunately, our species continues to be obedient to that command.

Psychological mysticism can be seen as a necessary correction to both dualistic notions. First, whatever the name we give to the mysterious Sacred Source of the universe, that Source is perceived to be within creation, within the very molecules of all matter. The created order is of the same *essence* as its Sacred Source. Second, psychological mysticism imagines our species to be an organic part of Nature and a continuous, unbroken connection to the Sacred Source itself. We now know that our very bodies consist of the same elements as the Cosmos itself. We are indeed the stuff of the stars!

These corrections to the long-held dualisms are enabling us to imagine that we are a vital part of an interrelated, interconnected, and interdependent sacred web of being. Our awareness that we are no longer separate from the Sacred Source, or from Nature, or from each other, has given birth to the lovely mystical phrase *Same/Same, Yet Different.* We share the same *essence* with all else, only in a different *form.* We are of the same *essence* as our Sacred Source, only in a different *form.* We are of the same *essence* as the planets and stars, only in a different *form.* We are of the same *essence* as our human and other-than-human beings, only in different *forms.*

A psychological mystical perspective builds necessary bridges across all our divides and divisions. In this liminal time between meaningful myths, psychological mysticism could serve as a healing bridge to our religious, cultural, and political future.

In *The Dream of the Cosmos: A Quest for the Soul,* Jungian analyst Anne Baring writes, "The insight that divinity is present in every single atom of life is precisely what has been missing in our concept of God and it is this which has led to the split between spirit and nature and, ultimately, to that between religion and science as well as to our growing capacity to inflict destruction on each other and on planetary life." Baring is one of numerous reflective authors who envision a hopeful new story, the cosmic story that continues to unfold, along with an unfolding of human consciousness. "Surely," she writes, "we are meant to evolve further, to bring into being not only a technology which can facilitate space travel, but a consciousness which can grow beyond tribal enmities and can open itself to the awareness that we all belong to a greater life: the life of this planet and beyond that, the life of the Cosmos" (Baring 2020:437-438).

Paralleling Baring's *The Dream of the Cosmos*, Thomas Berry, Roman Catholic priest, cultural historian, and self-described ecotheologian, authored *The Dream of the Earth, The Universe Story* (coauthor Brian Swimme), and *Evening Thoughts*. Berry is known for his phrase "The New Story," meaning the emerging story described in these pages. His memorable observation that "the universe is a communion of subjects, not a collection of objects" has helped to redeem the traditional monotheistic creation story, which gave the impression that the universe and Earth were unimportant backdrops for the whims of the human species. In the 17th century, Rene Descartes reinforced that unfortunate perspective when he concluded that the universe is composed simply of "mind and mechanism." Berry writes, "In this single stroke, he (Descartes) devitalized the planet and all its living creatures, with the exception of the human" (Berry 2006:17-18).

Psychological mysticism embraces the depth psychological perspective, the modern scientific insights, and centuries of mystical knowledge that we are a vital part of an animated Cosmos.

Australian author and professor David Tacy writes about the postmodern efforts to recover the sense of the Cosmos as alive and animated. He notes that all indigenous cultures have believed that the world is animated and alive with spiritual powers. Tacy says that depth psychology and science "are making inroads into the reanimation of the world ... by showing that the world is a holographic cosmos and not merely a collection of objects," the latter phrase borrowed from Thomas Berry (Tacy 2020:8). In his book *The Postsecular Sacred*, Tacy covers many of the themes offered in these pages on psychological mysticism. He writes, "The mystical speaks directly to postsecular conditions because it is non-clerical, immediate and transformative. The mystical is not dogmatic or assertive but receptive and open to sacredness of the ordinary" (Ibid.).

The psychological mystical path leads to an experiential appreciation of our unity with all things visible and invisible, a unity that also preserves our individuality. So intimate is one's connection with all that is, one can say:

> *Although I am not you, neither am I other than you; although I am not the Earth, neither am I other than the Earth; and when I look at the night sky with its billions of stars, although I am not the stars, neither am I other than the stars* (Wright, 2021:105).

Furthermore, on the psychological mystical path, one discovers the most mysterious, and the most humbling, aspects of the divine/human relationship: *Although I am not the Mystery we have named gods, goddesses, and God, neither am I other than the Mystery at the heart of matter* (Ibid.).

Psychological mysticism preserves the great secret: *We are already one with the Sacred Source.* We don't have to grit our teeth and work to make that happen. We are invited to trust what is and to live responsibly *as if* this is our nature and destiny. We share a collective continuity and inheritance, not only with our human ancestors, but with all forms of biological life and, even more astounding, with the matter of the cosmos in its 13.8 billion-year unfolding. Jung used the metaphor of the collective unconscious to speak of this metapersonal dimension to which we have access and, more importantly, which seems to seek out human consciousness as its manifestation and voice.

All of this means that Life will win out. It will continue its faithful and forceful unfolding as it has been doing for billions of years, for what we call eternity. With the gift of mystical consciousness, we are privileged to participate in that unfolding as cocreators. We can also neglect that privilege, to our detriment, yet Life will continue its mysterious flow (Wright 2021:105-06).

May we know that we are born mystics
Grounded, Embodied
Attuned to the numinous presences and powers
At the heart of the universe or universes
May we know that we are the stuff of the Cosmos
Neither greater than nor lesser than all else
And that all is holy.
May we see ourselves as threshold dwellers
Between the visible and invisible, conscious and unconscious
And from that mysterious intersection
May we live with passion and compassion
Our twin offerings
For the privilege of our sojourn.
And may we remember to bow seven times a day
Or seventy times seven.
(Wright 2021:151)

CHAPTER FOUR

AUTOPSY OF GOD THE FATHER

No yearning for an afterlife, no looking beyond,
no belittling death,
simply serving earth, the universe, and each other
as the gods intended.
(Wright, inspired by poems from Rilke's *Book of Hours*)

For the second half of my life, I have been performing a psychological autopsy on the mysteries we have named gods, goddesses, and God, particularly the God of Abraham. It is time to write the autopsy report.

I took on the autopsy task from a dream I had when I was 38 years old. The dream and my extended commentary can be found in the "Afterword" in the first volume of this trilogy, *Reimagining God and Religion*. The dream and some of the commentary can also be found in the "Introduction" of this volume.

The dream:

> My father has died, and we are standing beside the casket at the gravesite. A disembodied voice

> announces that there cannot be a burial until an autopsy is performed. I reach for the casket to brush off some of the ice/snow around the edges while asking, "Is this okay?" The voice replies, "Sure."

This was my initial dream I took to my analytic session with my Jungian psychoanalyst 45 years ago. In a mysterious way in Jungian analysis, initial dreams often speak to the particular issues and psychological complexes that are seeking consciousness. Such was the case for me.

At the time, I was a Presbyterian minister serving my third parish just outside New York City. I had consulted the analyst to work with numerous personal relational issues, including my continuing conflicted feelings about my religious vocation. My analysis focused on the "death of my father" in its many meanings—the early death of my personal father and my unresolved grief; the challenging relationships as a father and husband; my role as a spiritual father in my work as pastor and spiritual guide; and the claiming of my own personal authority as a good father to myself.

However, another father issue prompted performing the autopsy. Unknown and unforeseen by me at the time, yet apparently clear to the unconscious and dream-giver, the dream seemed to anticipate for me the death, grief, and autopsy of the *Father-God* and *Heavenly Father* images.

Of the several psychological complexes addressed in my first analysis, it has been my history, emotions, and concerns around religion and god, my *god complex*, that have been the most significant and enduring. Complexes are the internalized stories we tell ourselves about the stories we have learned about significant aspects of human life. Whether or not we consider ourselves to be religious, each of us has a *god complex*, a god-story, an internalized, emotionally charged story about the mysteries our species has named gods, goddesses, and God. The decisive question is the degree to which the story is conscious or unconscious. If a complex remains unconscious and unexamined, especially over a long period of time, we might say that the complex *has us*, meaning it affects our attitudes and behavior in unhealthy ways.

Over the years in lectures and on retreats and pilgrimages, I have publicly confessed my lifelong obsession with god and religion. Here is some of that history, some of my god-story.

When I was a young boy, I fell in love with the God-image of Christianity. It was a common, even expected, occurrence in the conservative, evangelical Christian tradition in which I was born and reared. Over the years, I have also fallen out of love with images of god numerous times, only to fall more deeply in love with the mystical depths of this mysterious universe and the mystical depths of the human psyche or soul. The love cycle with god and religion has repeated itself multiple times. Similar love cycles have revolved around the people, projects, ideas, and enthusiasms with whom I have fallen in love, out of love, and through love to ever deeper dimensions of the mystery we call love.

I also fell in love with Jesus at a very early age. Jesus was my superhero. He could walk on water, magically heal the sick, and he told fascinating stories. I liked the "photographs" of Jesus holding little children surrounded by sheep. They made me feel safe. I was convinced that he loved me and my family and friends. To use the idiom of our day—what's not to love about such a person?

My childhood love for Jesus and the Christian god-image began to waver as my view of the physical world widened, and as I encountered people different from my small, conservative, parochial, mostly white network of family and friends. The image of God as a hybrid of Superman and Santa Claus was no longer adequate. The images of a supersized human in a long flowing robe and beard, sitting on a cloud and extending his powerful hand on the Sistine ceiling, were no longer consistent with everything I was learning about the universe. The notion that my Christian tribe had some exclusive claim to truth was also problematic.

Week after week we were fed a diet of "Jesus Saves," including the belief in Jesus as the only way to God and Heaven. Being a faithful Christian also meant that we had to convert all others (the whole world) to our way of thinking/believing. At some fundamental (pun intended) level, I knew that something was wrong with that picture, yet I had no other legitimate picture to replace it.

By early adulthood, my conflicted feelings for god, Jesus, religion, and church had grown more intense. I had thought that entering theological seminary would be the solution, yet after one year of Hebrew, Greek, and the history of Christian doctrine and creeds, I knew that I had deceived myself. I withdrew from seminary to lick my wounds. After three years, and still conflicted, I returned to complete seminary training and embarked on a pastoral career.

Over the years, I have tried various treatment plans to get over my obsession with god and religion. I tried getting an education wider than the narrow religious education of my church family. I became a professional student. Like the Jonah of old, I also attempted to run away from a deep sense of religious calling by trying other professions. I even tried various kinds of psychotherapy, but religion and god were seldom addressed. My obsession seemed untreatable.

At midlife, I tried to address my obsession with god and religion by entering analysis with the Jungian psychoanalyst mentioned earlier. However, that only made my preoccupation with god and religion more intense—not less so! Rather than helping me *get over* my obsession, Jungian analysis and the worldview of Jungian Psychology did aid me in *getting under* what I considered my malady.

Underneath what I called my obsession, I discovered new meanings of the mysteries we have named gods, goddesses, and *God,* and a deeper appreciation for what Jung and his psychology calls the religious instinct. Much of the energy of my *god complex* has been channeled into my passion for work as a Jungian psychoanalyst, teaching, leading retreats and pilgrimages to numinous places around the world, and writing. The autopsy report suggests that my obsession remains intact, thankfully. To borrow a phrase from Jung, I now refer to the obsession as my "creative illness." Overall, I believe it has served me well.

There is no better way to express the experience of my dream than to say that the *image of God the Father* of my religious childhood died, and it died long before I was able to acknowledge the death consciously. As I have listened to this personal dream over the years, and as I have listened to the dreams and stories of many others, I believe the dream has collective meanings as well. I believe that there are countless others gathered around the metaphorical gravesite in various stages of unconscious grief due to the death of the monotheistic myth and its core image of God (Wright 2018:29ff).

Considering the autopsy, the date of the death of the monotheistic myth and its image of God seems uncertain, although likely calculated in centuries, even before Galileo, Copernicus, and Kepler provided their nails for the heavenly coffin. To extend the metaphor, it appears it was a slow death as various life-support measures were employed to keep from facing the inevitable. Psychologically, the pathological aspects of monotheism and the image of God the Father continue to be kept alive by patriarchal attitudes and behaviors. The current authoritarian political movements in the United States and in numerous other nations are prime examples of regressive, patriarchal religion disguised as politics.

On examination of the deceased, the causes of death are both physical and psychological. Physically, the religious myth was based on a three-tiered view of the universe that became untenable, except through denial and willful ignorance of science. Also, the myth was dualistic from the beginning, elevating heaven over Earth, and viewing the Earth and its resources as objects to be consumed. In the highly spiritualized myth, the Earth was considered to be a place of exile and punishment. Furthermore, we are still trying to recover from the monotheistic myth's devaluation of women, the feminine principle, the human body, and sexuality.

When I remember my childhood image of God as a personified, supernatural, interventionist, male Being dwelling outside and beyond the physical universe (i.e., a theistic Being), I can imagine various causes of his death:

- He died of a broken heart watching his children fight over who was his favorite tribe.
- He was killed over and over again by friendly fire, caught in the middle of wars he never wanted, never condoned, never blessed.
- He was suffocated to death by rigid, airtight creeds and dogma.
- He died of loneliness, exiled far from the Earth, from animals, and from humans he dearly loved.
- He died from caregiver's burnout, always being asked for favors, and seldom asked what he wanted, how he was feeling, or what his hopes for the world were.

- Or, perhaps he died of natural causes as part of the universal life-death-rebirth cycle he created, a cycle applicable also to him and to future god-images.
- Or, even more likely, the symbol G-O-D died because it ceased to be a symbol and became a literal, personified, male Being, rather than a connection to unnamable mysteries at the heart of being itself.

This brings us back to the psychological autopsy of God the Father. These essays, and the trilogy as a whole, have established the psychological perspective that our god-images are birthed through the human imagination in concert with the dynamics of psychological projection. The names, images, and metaphors that we assign to numinous experiences are our efforts to understand our place and purpose in the mysterious universe in which we find ourselves. *Our gods, then, are internal, intrapsychic experiences, images, energies, and resources that serve the human personality to embrace its organic connection to the Sacred Source and to all else. Religions are meant to be the communities and rituals that serve this sacred purpose.*

When god-images are literalized as external, supernatural beings, they lose their symbolic capacity. They slowly die. The image of God the Father died due to literalism and the failure of the religious imagination to nurture what it had birthed. Our god-images have not been allowed to develop and evolve. Metaphorically, our species has birthed gods and exported them beyond the physical world. Separated from the care and the intimacy of the human psyche/soul, our gods have suffered from a failure to thrive. And so has the human soul.

Imagination is our most important psychological and spiritual faculty. It is nature's gift by which we birth our gods and religions, as well as all of our scientific advances and works of art. It was the human imagination that permitted our ancestors to personify their numinous experiences as gods and goddesses who occupied Mount Olympus, Mount Sinai, and a metaphysical Heaven. Yet, it was the failure of the religious imagination that left them there to die.

As Jung explored the internal operating systems (IOS) of the internal, invisible world, he turned to the ancient art of Alchemy with its emphasis on the imagination to link the opposites of life. Jung identified a uniting principle in alchemy, and its name was "*imaginatio*" (Stein 2017:18). Jung writes, "The concept of *imaginatio* is perhaps the most important key to the understanding of the opus" (Jung 1952/1970:396). Murray Stein extends that perspective: "Imagination would be the key to open the windows of perception to the *unus mundus,* the creation of a state of consciousness that does not divide but holds together what has been sundered and kept apart, inner and outer, above and below ... *Imaginatio* is the way the self perceives the world, as *unus mundus ...*" (Stein, 2017:18).

Psychological mysticism promotes the religious imagination as the key to unlock the closed, exclusive doors of our religious past and to open the doors to a more creative, inclusive, religious future. There have never been literal, supernatural beings hovering over the physical world issuing divine decrees or immutable laws, or granting favors or promised land, or demanding sacrifices or devotion. Likewise, there is no remote divinity that helps us to win ballgames or political races or wars. To say otherwise is delusional thinking. It is a failure of the religious imagination. It is deadly. Literalism kills.

The image of God the Father as a supernatural, interventionist Being, who dwells outside the physical world and the human psyche, is a psychological delusion. Throughout the history of our species, all of our gods have been and remain *psychic images rather than literal supernatural beings.* The prevailing notion that God is a literal supernatural Being remains our species' most dangerous delusion. We must bury that image and mourn its death.

The psychological autopsy of the death of God the Father supports the repeated warning throughout this trilogy: *As long as our deities and devils are perceived to be outside the physical world and beyond the human psyche, we will continue to do great harm to ourselves, to each other, and to our beautiful nest.*

As indicated in the opening sentence of this essay, the autopsy in my dream has been taking shape for 45 years. Far from being a morbid activity, it has been life-affirming and life-giving. Autopsies are performed on the occasion of death, yet they are always done to resource the living. Through teaching and writing, I have joined many others who are imagining a new religious story that begs to be told.

The new story is slowly taking shape. It invites the best of our imagination in general and our religious imagination in particular. It begins with welcoming our gods back home to the human psyche, where they were birthed, where they belong, and where they can serve as resources for passionate and compassionate living. The following essay imagines that homecoming.

CHAPTER FIVE

WELCOMING OUR GODS BACK HOME

All will come again into its strength:
the fields undivided, the trees towering
and the walls built low.
And in the valleys
people as strong and varied as the land.
And no churches, temples, and mosques
where the gods are imprisoned and lamented
like trapped and wounded animals.
(Wright, inspired by poems from Rilke's *Book of Hours*)

Perhaps the most important religious question of the 20th century was asked by a psychologist rather than a theologian or philosopher. Pondering our species' many gods and religions over the centuries, Carl Gustav Jung asked rhetorically, "Where did the Greek gods and goddesses go when they left Mount Olympus" (Jung 1967:54)? His psychological answer was that they disappeared into the unconscious and from there they have continued to influence consciousness in all manner of ways, including pathological symptoms.

Jung would go on to expand his provocative perspective by proposing that the human psyche and imagination are the birthplace of our gods and religions and their original metaphorical home. Considering Jung's massive corpus of writing, Jungian analyst John Dourley notes, "The ... recalling of the Gods to their psychogenetic origin and the responsibility of dealing with them there is the defining characteristic and psychological culmination of Jung's psychology" (Dourley 2010:48; Wright 2018:73).

With Jung's psychological insights on god-images and religions, our species quietly moved from a Theological Age to a Psychological Age. Jung's psychological insights on the birthplace of the gods and religions have proven to be a Copernican shift from what Marcus Borg called an *earlier religious paradigm* toward an *emerging religious paradigm* (Borg 2006:14-26). However, that shift remains largely unacknowledged in theological, religious, and cultural circles. The volumes in this trilogy have encouraged consciousness of that shift and of the personal and collective meanings, including the implications for the future of our species. The religious/spiritual implications of this subtle move are tremendous and perhaps salvific.

Every few weeks I receive a notice on my smartphone that "Your IOS will be updated tonight," and the next morning I receive a notice that my phone has been updated. Because I am technologically challenged, until recently I had no idea what was being done to my phone, or what "IOS" meant. When I asked my children, they informed me that IOS means Internal Operating Systems and that very smart people are forever updating our phones, as well as updating our many other technological toys. I am grateful for such people.

What caught my imagination was the phrase *Internal Operating Systems* as it could be applied to depth psychology and religion. Carl Jung became fascinated with the internal operating systems of the human psyche/soul and with the operations of mind/body/spirit. He spent his life updating and revising his psychological system, including a new language—archetypes, archetypal unconscious, complexes, shadow, psychological types, projection, the ego-Self relationship, etc. Because of his pioneering work, we now know the human psyche as an amazing combination of internal operating systems that spill over and affect all other operating systems, including religion.

Our religions and religious institutions also have internal operating systems. Most human endeavors—physics, medicine, astronomy and other sciences, the arts, and various technological fields—continue to thrive because of their regular IOS updates. Not so for our religions and religious institutions.

Historically, religion and the religious imagination have been reluctant to update their internal operating systems. Thay have been held captive by a combination of nostalgia, fear, ignorance, and most dangerous of all, willful ignorance. E. O. Wilson offers a fair assessment of our religious history in his book, *The Meaning of Human Existence*. He notes that religions have been a source of inspiration, comfort, and hope for millions throughout our relatively young history as a species. Then he exposes the underbelly of religion: "The great religions are also, and tragically, sources of ceaseless and unnecessary suffering. They are impediments to the grasp of reality needed to solve most social problems in the real world. Their exquisite human flaw is *tribalism*. … The true cause of hate and violence is faith versus faith.

… Faith is the one thing that makes otherwise good people do bad things." (Wilson 2014:150-52,177). When considered in their entirety, religions have impeded human consciousness and human thriving.

C. G. Jung directed his professional life to this dangerous deficit. With his passion both for religion and psychology, he explored the inner workings of both disciplines and their intimate connections. His work and writings bridge the great gap between religion and science, perhaps as no other work before or since. As he established the internal operating systems of the human psyche, he was simultaneously providing updates on the IOS of religion and religious institutions.

Jung's most profound and far-reaching update on religion and religious experience is the subject before us—*the recognition that our gods are internal, intrapsychic experiences, images, energies, and resources rather than external beings.* This insight may well prove to be the inner Copernican Revolution that mirrors the external one of the 15th century (Copernicus, 1473-1543). Jung's insight is at the heart of the emerging story, the emerging myth that updates the earlier theistic myths that were at their core dependent on external, supernatural, interventionist beings.

Welcoming Our Gods Back Home proposes that our modern psychospiritual task will involve retrieving our personified, anthropomorphized, and literalized deities and devils from their external domains of Heaven and Hell, and returning them to the human psyche and imagination, where they originated and where they belong. Then, and likely only then, will we reclaim ethical responsibility for our creative and destructive capacities we formerly assigned to external divine and devilish beings. Until then, the divisions, destruction, and deaths that we visit on each other, and on our Earth home, will most likely continue and increase. Or, as noted repeatedly throughout these three volumes: *As long as our gods are perceived to be supernatural beings beyond the physical world in a metaphysical domain and outside the human psyche, our species will continue to do great harm to each other, to ourselves, and to our global nest.*

At present, the welcoming committee for the homecoming of our gods may seem relatively small. Most people continue to favor the view that an external, supernatural, interventionist, divine Being (God) dropped down religious truths from a metaphysical realm. That all-good, all-powerful, all-knowing Being is opposed by another personified Being, Satan, or the Devil. While such images were consistent with an earlier level of human consciousness, they are no longer adequate given what we know about our universe, visible and invisible. The premodern viewpoint has been perpetuated by what Jung called a systematic blindness that our gods are wholly *outside* man (Jung 1934b:100). Slowly, ever so slowly, human consciousness in general, and religious consciousness in particular, have evolved sufficiently to recognize that our deities and devils are internal, intrapsychic experiences, images, energies, and resources rather than external supernatural beings. This psychological perspective bears repeating—*to recognize that our gods are internal, intrapsychic experiences, images, energies, and resources, rather than external beings.*

Drawing on the Sufi tradition, I propose:

There is no god
except the experience of god
so says Sufi mystical wisdom
Wisdom sorely needed in a time
when the old deities in the top rung
of a three-tiered universe
have either died or retired
Leaving heaven-hungry humans
clinging to dogmatic life rafts
barely afloat in a turbulent institutional sea.
(Wright 2021:13)

With the dawn of the Psychological Age, the archetypal foundations of a new god-story, a new religious myth, came into view. Jung was among the first to take notice of that subtle archetypal shift beneath the multiple collective traumas of the 20th century. The outlines of a new story, a new collective myth, continue to emerge as visionaries from many human disciplines, especially astronomers, astrophysicists, quantum physicists, and other scientists have joined its telling. The new story, the new myth, will expand and deepen what it means to be religious. Yet, even deeper, the new story will guide us toward what it means to be *human*—to be *human* in an interconnected, interrelated, interdependent universe.

The new story/myth will include what we now know about the expansive, expanding physical universe and the vast, invisible, psychological universe. In the last century, as scientists were exploring the outer, visible, physical universe, Carl Jung and others were exploring the inner, invisible psychological universe. In terms of their vastness, mystery, and continuing revelation, the two universes may be thought of as mirror images of each other. Jungian analyst Jolande Jacobi, writes about the archetypal psyche, "The collective unconscious consists of an unlimited sum of fundamental psychic conditions accumulated over millions of years, a realm of immeasurable breadth and depth. ... It is the inner equivalent of creation, an inner cosmos as infinite as the cosmos outside us" (Jacobi 1971:59). Brian Swimme, Professor of Mathematics and Evolutionary Cosmology and author of *Cosmogenesis*, reminds us that we are the first generation to know the large-scale structure of the universe. Our Milky Way galaxy is but one of an estimated 2 trillion galaxies, each with millions of stars. He writes that we are the present tense of an expanding universe. We are cosmological beings as well as human beings.

Our human story is part of a much larger story, and both stories continue to expand and unfold.

This trilogy is offered as a contribution to that continuing story, to the *emerging myth* of what it means to be human in an interrelated, interconnected, interdependent universe. As noted elsewhere, it will likely take many generations for a fully formed myth to be identified. In the meantime, we are tasked with imagining possible meanings, attitudes, and behaviors that will be required of our reflective species. As we wait for a new collective myth, we can *practice the future* by living *as if* it is already here, *as if* we are a vital part of an interconnected, interrelated, interdependent universe.

Why have we kept our gods
so remote for so long
And made our religions so difficult
and for so few
Would it not be more human
and humane and divine
to live *as if* we are the gods
we have birthed
And the devils we have shunned
Or is that asking too much
of our religious pathology
and our adolescence as a species?
(Wright 2021:16-17)

Practicing the future begins metaphorically with *welcoming our gods back home, where they were birthed and where they belong.* Having them back home on Earth, within matter, and within the human psyche, will enable closer mirroring, monitoring, and responsibly owning our capacities for great creativity and great destruction, for great good and great evil. Psychologically, we share these twin capacities with Nature itself, with the additional gift of reflective consciousness to mediate both. Welcoming the gods back home to the human psyche could ensure that we have a future.

In general, our species has taken legitimate pride in our amazing gifts of creativity, even though we have often ignored the possible evil side effects, both physical and ethical. The creation of weapons of mass destruction is a prime example. Our capacities for care and compassion have been visible and laudable, yet we have denied our equally unspeakable capacities for evil. Our capacity for evil has taken many forms, including cruelty, hate, prejudice, and murderous elimination of other humans who threaten our security or way of life, or who oppose our images of gods that we feel obliged to defend.

These pages are being written the morning after the June 22, 2025, bombing of the Iranian nuclear facilities by the United States, adding to the long-running religious wars initiated and perpetuated by monotheistic madness (Wright 2018:39-58). When our gods are perceived to be external, supernatural Beings located out of sight in the heavenly beyond, any individual, religious group, or nation can claim divine favoritism or validation. External theistic Gods and their religions have been favorite hiding places for the human shadow. Sadly, on battlefields in the Middle East and around the world, we continue to offer human blood sacrifices to those external Gods.

Blood sacrifices have played a central role in the religious histories of our species. One of the most familiar stories of sacrifice concerns God's call to Abraham to sacrifice his son, Isaac. In the last minute, God provides a sacrificial lamb instead (Genesis 22:1-19).

This difficult story is most often interpreted as a test of Abraham's faith in the monotheistic Father-God, who is still referenced as the God of Abraham.

There have been innumerable interpretations of this biblical story that attempt to show the monotheistic God-image in a more favorable light. One such philosophical or symbolic interpretation suggests that Isaac—Abraham and Sarah's only son—represented Abraham's connection to the past, and to Abraham's future, with the promise that he would be the "father of many nations." Symbolically, God the Father was asking Abraham to sacrifice a past that he could not relive and a future that he could not control. This, of course, is the human situation and predicament; we cannot undo our past or control our future. We are asked to sacrifice our past and future by living the present moment with faith/trust. The Christian story adds hope and love (I Corinthians 13).

Not only must we, like Abraham, sacrifice a past that we cannot undo and a future we cannot control, this trilogy calls for an even greater sacrifice—that is, the sacrifice of Abraham's God, or more precisely, Abraham's image of God as an external, supernatural, interventionist Being. Until that sacrifice can be offered by a significant number of Jews, Christians, and Muslims, the three major monotheistic religions will remain caught in repeated cycles of monotheistic madness. The blood sacrifices of young warriors and innocent children and adults will likely continue on the battlefields of the world.

The new myth will also require another related sacrifice. We must sacrifice the practice of psychological scapegoating. Scapegoating has a long history. It was instituted as a religious ritual in the early history of monotheism. With priestly help, the sins of the people were ritually placed on a goat or sheep. Sometimes the animal was then slaughtered as a blood sacrifice to God or sent out into the wilderness to die.

The effectiveness of the ritual in dealing with the sins of the people could be debated. What is not debatable are the devastating results of modern-day scapegoating—blaming, demeaning, or shaming others for the very things we refuse to face in ourselves. A form of psychological projection, scapegoating is an attempt to hide from our unwanted shadow by placing it on someone else. The practice of scapegoating is so common it is considered normal. For example, our current political arrangements operate as "sanctioned scapegoat systems" whereby any problem, failure, or enemy lies in the other person, the other political party, or the other nation. The initial chapter of this volume, "Speaking to the Political Elephant in the Room," addresses this familiar way of dealing with the human shadow.

In the final analysis, to welcome our gods back home means *to come back home to ourselves*, to those parts of ourselves that were cast away to external deities and to theological doctrines and dualisms that divided heaven and Earth, divine and human, spirit and matter. Psychological mysticism provides a path to come home to ourselves, to our home in the natural world rather than in a supernatural world populated with supernatural beings. Welcoming our gods back home also means retrieving the personal shadow and collective shadow that we attribute to an external devil or that we assign to those individuals and nations who mirror our own duplicity. It means to bear the opposites of life within our own being, within our own soul, rather than exporting them to external beings or to our neighbors or enemies. Employing the archetypal image of *atonement* that remains central to the earlier monotheistic paradigm, welcoming our gods back home will allow fresh meanings of at-one-ment (atonement) with ourselves.

The earlier myth or religious paradigm proposes that, due to original sin, we were radically separated from God and, therefore, from the deepest parts of ourselves and from the Earth itself. That inherent separation required some method of reconciliation or atonement, ranging from religious rituals and blood sacrifices, to the substitutionary blood sacrifice of Jesus in the Christian myth. Jesus is considered to be the human scapegoat for sins, the necessary atonement. Again, the effectiveness of scapegoat Christology could be debated. Psychologically, all too often giving our sins to Jesus means repressing the human shadow that then reappears in another form.

Psychological mysticism proposes a *new story*, a story of *connection* rather than *separation*. The new story preserves our continuing connection to the source of life that burst into being 14 billion years ago. With our current knowledge of the visible and invisible aspects of the Cosmos, we now know that we are a vital part of the interconnected, interrelated, interdependent web of being. We are at-one-with our origins, by whatever name(s) we choose to describe the mysteries at the heart of the universe. We are at-one-with the Earth. We are at-one-with all others, human and other than human. This is the new story. No *atonement* is needed.

Indeed,
why does it take a lifetime
to come Home to ourselves
when we live so close?
(Wright 2021:117-119)

Welcoming our gods back home also provides fresh meanings to the archetypal image of *incarnation*. The image of incarnation (gods in human flesh) has emerged into collective consciousness numerous times over religious history, most notably 2,000 years ago in the Christian story/myth. In the Christian imagination, the mystical teacher Jesus became the recipient of godlike projections from the imagination of his followers. Those projections gave rise to the mistaken name, *Jesus Christ,* as if Christ were the last name of Jesus.

Unable to recognize their idealizations of Jesus as psychological projections, and unable to withdraw and to internalize them, Jesus' disciples, the Apostle Paul, and the early church fathers declared him to be God incarnate. Jesus was considered to be *The Incarnation,* rather than a human being through whom the archetypal image of Christ was manifest. In the popular Christian mind, Jesus remains the human scapegoat for sins. He was lifted off the Earth to dwell alongside God the Father in a remote metaphysical realm until his future return. This deification further separated divine and human, spirit and matter, even as it supposedly celebrated "God with us."

Two chapters in Volume One of this series are devoted to a thorough depth psychological exploration of how and why the historical Jesus became known mistakenly as *Jesus Christ.* Drawing on the insights of Analytical Psychology, the chapters explore the distinction between history and myth and, to paraphrase Jung, *the necessity of withdrawing projections from the historical or metaphysical Jesus in order for the archetypal Christ to incarnate more fully in and through us, as it did in and through Jesus* (Jung 1958:725; Wright 2018:121). As heretical as it may sound, the new myth will also require a sacrifice of the name *Jesus Christ* so that we can recover the value of the mystical teachings of the historical Jesus, and recover the archetypal image of Christ as an inner resource. Welcoming our gods back home will recover the meaning of incarnation as a universal psychospiritual task, rather than limiting it to one historical person. Jung concludes, "… the myth of the necessary incarnation of God—the essence of the Christian message—can then be understood as man's confrontation with the opposites and their synthesis in the self, the wholeness of personality" (Jung 1965: p. 338).

(See Chapters Six and Seven of *Reimagining God and Religion*, pp. 97-136, for an in-depth psychological review of this critical theme.)

Welcoming our gods back home, where they were birthed and where they belong, will also return value to the human body as a sacred vessel. Monotheistic religions and texts have denied the importance of the body and, more severely, have denigrated and pathologized the body's natural sexual instincts and expressions. The body has been seen as an enemy to the experiences of the holy rather than its closest friend. As part of the Earth itself, the body is the finest-tuned mystical instrument available to us. We remember that a numinous encounter initiates a bodily response followed by intense emotion. Psychological mysticism and the new story honor the body as the first detector and responder to the nearness of the sacred.

In the new story, our bodies and psyches are the human channels and conduits of the Sacred Source itself. Our bodies and psyches are the finely tuned instruments of incarnation. Psychologically, we are also the organic openings through which the mystery of consciousness enters the visible world. The mystical poet Rabindranath Tagore asks, *what wants to enter the world through me now* (Tagore 2020:107)? This question validates the psychological mystical perspective before us. The question is worthy of our regular inquiry: *what wants to enter the world through me now?* Mary Oliver issues a similar challenge when she asks, "Tell me, what is it you plan to do with your one wild and precious life" (Oliver 1992:94)? James Hollis speaks to these questions in the context of the individuation process. He writes, "All of us are humble carriers of the spark of life and the project of individuation. Individuation does not mean a fatuous, narcissistic self-absorption but rather a submission to what wants to enter the world through us" (Hollis 2020:132).

With our gods back home, the vital religious question presented to us is not, *Do you believe in the gods of your ancestors?* The more relevant questions are: *Will you live responsibly the deity-like and devil-like capacities within your own self; within your own religious tribe; within your own political tribe; within your own community and nation?*

With our gods back home, the experience and practice of *prayer* takes on profound significance. Because we are *home to* and *conduits for* the Sacred Source of life, when we pray, we are acknowledging and accessing the resources for life already close at hand, close to our folded hands, as it were. Prayer is an act of trust. The energies and resources that we need in the moment are already available to us for celebrating life and facing difficult challenges. In the new story, prayer is not a summons of a remote deity but of the deity at the heart of matter of which we are an organic part. Prayer is also not a plea for an external god to clean up the messes of our own making.

Trusting our at-one-ment with the Sacred Source of the universe, as well as with all else, fortifies the ego to be a confident, courageous, and compassionate channel, whether for ourselves or for another. Drawing on a favorite depth psychological image, each of us has ready access to the great underground stream. The disciplines of prayer, meditation, journaling, dreamwork, art, yoga and other body disciplines, as well as numerous other practices, are the various wells we descend to tap the Water of Life within.

According to Jungian analyst Robert Johnson, "The Water of Life" was one of Jung's favorite stories. Johnson often told the story himself. The story concludes with some version of "There is always life-giving water available, if one knows where to search, and if one searches with the right attitude."

Depth psychology and modern science suggest that the energies and attitudes that we put out into the *psychological field* may have an effect on others in the field. We know this to be true when we can feel various energies between us and others. Our unspoken attitudes, as well as our bodies, communicate powerful messages. To pray affirms that we are part of an interconnected, interrelated, and interdependent web of being, and that we are the conduits and channels for creativity and compassion.

To be prayerful also means to be aware when we are channeling our less desirable qualities, our ever-present shadow, which also resides in our inner house. Buddhist scholar and social activist Joanna Macy reminds us, "If we're all connected enough to belong to one another, then we're connected enough to hurt one another—a lot (Macy 2020:4). Our shadow needs to stay at home, to be a homebody. When our shadow is tempted to visit someone else, there is usually a fear involved. Naming the fear usually keeps the shadow at home, where it can get home care. As I mentioned in the first chapter, "Speaking to the Political Elephant in the Room," taking responsibility for our shadow may be the one best thing we can do for the peace of the world and for our own peace of mind.

Again, welcoming our gods back home means simultaneously coming home to ourselves. Poet Derek Walcott pictures that homecoming:

The time will come
when, with elation,
you will greet yourself arriving
at your own door, in your own mirror,
and each will smile at the other's welcome,

and say, sit here. Eat.
You will love again the stranger who was your self.
Give wine. Give bread. Give back your heart
to itself, to the stranger who has loved you

all your life, whom you ignored
for another, who knows you by heart.
Take down the love letters from the bookshelf,

the photographs, the desperate notes,
peel your own image from the mirror.
Sit. Feast on your life.
(Walcott 1986:328)

To reiterate: In the final analysis, to welcome our gods back home means *to come back home to ourselves*, to those parts of ourselves that were cast away to external deities, and to theological doctrines and dualisms that divided heaven and earth, divine and human, and spirit and matter. Welcoming our gods back home also means retrieving the personal shadow and collective shadow that we attribute to an external devil or that we assign to those individuals and nations who mirror our own duplicity.

I reached a similar conclusion in Volume One:

> Looking back from a place far down the evolutionary road, we may see the religions of the past as necessary stages along a twisting, labyrinthine path toward the realization that *we are, in fact, what we imaged our former deities and devils to be.* No, we will not see ourselves as little gods. Rather, we will accept our full humanity through whom both godly and demonic powers are manifest. Our species will come to recognize and own both our glory and gory, which were projected, necessarily so, onto external deities and devils. We will conclude that, in the wisdom of psyche, it was necessary to see our creative and destructive capacities in projected form until we could own them and manifest both responsibly. Squinting, that is as far as I can see (Wright 2018:193).

Now seven years later I am still squinting. Yet, what becomes clearer by the day is the necessity to bring depth psychological wisdom to our individual religious impulses as well as to our religious, political, and cultural collectives.

Carl Jung devoted his life and work to weaving the visible and invisible threads of a universal web of being that he identified as the *unus mundus*, the unified world. In his extensive work on alchemy, he quotes an alchemical source that describes the *unus mundus* as the "latent unity of the world" (Jung 1963:663). The unified world was the underlying basis for Jung's theory of synchronicity and the mystery of synchronistic experiences. The synchronistic principle "... suggests that there is an inter-connection or unity of causally unrelated events, and thus postulates a unitary aspect of being which can very well be described as the *unus mundus*" (Ibid:662).

Near the end of his life, Jung described his felt connection to the natural, unified world: "At times I feel as if I am spread out over the landscape and inside things, and am myself living in every tree, in the splashing of the waves, in the clouds and the animals that come and go, in the procession of the seasons. There is nothing ... with which I am not linked" (Jung 1965: p. 225-226).

Psychological mysticism imagines the individuation process as a gradual embrace of the unified world, the *unus mundus,* of which each person and all things are an organic part. Jung spoke clearly of the metaphorical, mystical embrace: "Individuation does not shut one out from the world, but gathers the world to oneself" (Jung 1960:432).

In his book, *Outside, Inside and All Around* Jungian psychoanalyst Murray Stein writes: "... we recognize that in its advanced stages the process of individuation leads to profound recognition of the unity of the world and the self (*unus mundus*), even while ego-consciousness continues at the same time to maintain clear boundaries and differences" (Stein 2017:14). Stein's description of the process of individuation echoes the mystical perspective spoken of in these volumes—*Same/Same, Yet Different.*

Psychological mysticism proposes that each of us has access to the reservoir of natural and human wisdom accumulated over millennia. The wisdom of the universe is not stored up in a metaphysical domain and dispensed by a heavenly parent. Wisdom is within the depths of life itself, within each of us, *in the deep innerness of all things* (Rilke). We are wired to that wisdom. It is our task and delight to make visible that wisdom and to be that wisdom. With consciousness we can contribute to that reservoir for future generations. The psychological word for the storehouse of wisdom is the unconscious. The unconscious is also the womb where our future life is gestating and from which our future will be birthed. We are privileged to be the midwives of the future.

In Volume Two, I included an imaginary email message from the Wisdom of the Universe to the travelers on the mystical path. That message from personified Wisdom concluded with:

> The doorway to Wisdom is close at hand. It is an inner doorway. You will locate that Wisdom deep within, underneath your fears and prejudices, and your need to be right and to win at all costs. You are better than that, you are wiser than that, and you are more creative than that. Go into your fears and through them. Just on the other side is that secret passageway. Enter there and you will come to a beautiful meadow out beyond right and wrong, beyond winning and losing, beyond red states and blue states, beyond liberal and conservative, and beyond all the divisions of your making. I will meet you there in that deep inner place. We can converse and decide how to go back into the outer world to create a less conflicted, less terror-filled life together. We need to do so. We must do so. We can do so. You and I working together (Wright 2021:139-145).

The quality of our future as a species will depend on individuals who are psychologically conscious participants in the interconnected, interrelated, interdependent, universal web of being, the *unus mundus*. With our gods back home in the human psyche, where they were birthed and where they belong, we are one step closer to realizing the unified world.

AFTERWORD

You, Great Mystery,
are the deep innerness of all things,
the last word that can never be spoken.
(Wright, inspired by poems from Rilke's *Book of Hours*)

I have come to the end of this latest writing project. As I reflect on my long professional career—teaching, speaking, listening, and writing—the words of Eliza Doolittle are especially appropriate and challenging.

Doolittle was the main character in George Bernard Shaw's 1913 play *Pygmalion* and its 1956 musical adaptation *My Fair Lady*. Expressing frustration to her romantic pursuers, she sings:

> Words! Words! Words!
> I'm so sick of words. I get words all day through
> First from him, now from you!
> Is that all you blighters can do?
> Show me! Show me!
> Don't talk of love lasting through time
> Make no undying vow. Show me now!

Sing me no song. Read me no rhyme
Don't waste my time, Show me!
Don't talk of June. Don't talk at all! Show me!
Never do I ever want to hear another word
There isn't one I haven't heard
Say one more and I'll scream
Don't wait until wrinkles and lines
Pop out all over my brow
Show me, Show me now!
(Lyrics by Alan Jay Lerner; see "Sources Cited")

As a teacher, minister, and psychoanalyst, I have spent my career speaking, writing, and listening to words. Or I could say, I have spent my career romancing words. I love words and their possible meanings, yet words are paradoxical. Words can reveal who we are, and words can conceal. With words we can become transparent and vulnerable. Words can also be a favorite hiding place. Words can create. Words can destroy.

The paradoxical character of language and words reveals itself in efforts to address the mysteries our species has named gods, goddesses, and God. It may be that more words have been written and spoken about religions and "God" than any other topic. I have contributed more than my share. And, yet, the mysteries remain. And so does our religious pathology.

The prophetess Eliza Doolittle reminds us that words must be balanced by deeds, by behaviors, by actions. Balance and harmony are the invisible dynamics, the internal operating systems, of the outer, physical universe. The same is true for the inner, psychological universe, which is the playground and workshop for our gods, for our capacities for great good and great evil. Imbalance and one-sidedness could be considered the original sin of the inner world.

The external world has cosmic laws in place to manage its balance. Each of us is responsible for balancing our internal world.

The metaphor—welcoming our gods back home—seeks to balance the overemphasis on god-images that have been external to physical life, the life of matter, and to the life of the human psyche. Equally, the metaphor sounds the alarm when god-images and their religions are too bright, too light, and too good, and neglect the human shadow and the human capacity for evil.

With our gods back home, perhaps we are one step closer to claiming responsibility for, and accountability for, our capacities for great good and great evil. If so, it will mean that our words and deeds will have been wed.

PSYCHOLOGICAL MYSTICISM IN VERSE

These poems by the author were first published throughout Volume Two, *A Mystical Path Less Traveled.* Some have been slightly revised.

I think of poetry as *round words* capable of holding multiple meanings. Poems are also verbal bridges connecting apparent opposites, giving birth to paradox, irony, and holy contradictions. Poetry may be our best language to express the inexpressible and to name the unnamable. Like music, poems invite recurring listening, and their images may take up residence and resonance in our soul (Wright 2021: 7-8).

god

There is no god
except the experience of god
so says Sufi mystical wisdom
Wisdom sorely needed in a time
when the old deities in the top rung
of a three-tiered universe
have either died or retired

Leaving heaven-hungry humans
clinging to dogmatic life rafts
barely afloat in a turbulent institutional sea.

What sounds like bad news portends
good news for those who no longer reside
in that collapsed universe
and for those who can no longer abide
a supernatural being
who has a favorite tribe
and only one son guarding the salvation gate
Creating an illusory shortage of divine water
requiring fences and secret creedal codes
Generating competition, division, and terror
and more and more weapons to protect one's god
and stories deemed sacred.

As long as our deities are supernatural beings
occupying an external metaphysical home
and intervening for our religious tribe
We will continue to do great harm
to others, ourselves, and our earth home
While doing a victory dance
in sanctuary, sports field, or political hall
proclaiming we are number one
while losers weep
and plan the next inevitable battle.

We continue to spill blood
over the stories we tell ourselves
about the gods we have created

and are obliged to defend
Excusing our cycles of violence and terror
while praying god's will be done
Or God bless America, or Allahu Akbar
before lying down for fitful sleep
We will to our children our unwillingness
to face our human fears disguised as faith
Their inheritance our unlived life.

Who will have the uncommon courage
to speak common sense to our common delusions
of external magical gods and magical books
How long will we export the responsibility
for our difficult human choices to a remote deity
or to a human pope, or to a dusty paper pope
created by the Bronze-age male psyche?

Was the reduction of the many gods and goddesses
to one supernatural male
revelation from heaven's heights
Or eruption from the human depths
of two-million-year-old fears of
shortages of god-goodies?

When will we accept that
all our gods and goddesses are
necessary symbols or metaphors
The supernatural, theistic, all-male God of Abraham
being no exception
How else can we explain so many gods
over so many years for so many peoples?

Meanwhile we humans remain innately conflicted
needing god-images to relate to the mysteries
in which we find ourselves
Yet preferring to possess the power
behind and beneath the image
When management of the mysteries
overrides trust of those mysteries
dogmatic religions are birthed
along with overt and covert terror.

Symbols and metaphors
provide a peek behind the veil
Protection from the blinding light
of the ineffable and unnamable
though we are compelled to keep trying
They remain the best medicine
for ego-inflated and power-hungry
individuals and religious tribes and nations
claiming to be founded by a god
with stamped coinage providing proof.

When symbolic gods are abandoned
to the trash heap of literalism
They become poisonous darts to the heart
and religious Kool-Aid dispensed by
self-appointed messiahs
Let us beware of any god that can be
possessed or owned or marketed
regardless of how many TV screens
are in the Sunday marketplace.

When the experiences of god are elevated
as the mystical norm
The remote gods
will be free to incarnate
Not once as rumored
but everywhere and everywhen
Every bush and person ablaze
with dazzling unquenchable light
The light of the world
no longer hidden under a bushel
as the mystical teacher proposed.

The god-experiences keep a-coming
moment by numinous moment
for those who have keen eyes
and discerning ears
They emerge not from theological heights
but from collective psychological depths
Where god-like powers and presences
actively plan their next excursion
through the thin curtain
Desiring even demanding their rightful place
in the human heart
and economy.

Why have we kept our gods
so remote for so long
And made our religions so difficult
and for so few
Would it not be more human
and humane and divine

to live *as if* we are the gods
we have created
And the devils we have shunned
Or is that asking too much
of our religious pathology
and our adolescence as a species?

This author is often accused
of using passionate, even angry words
when addressing the holy business of religion
Guilty as charged your honor
having been complicit in promoting
external supernatural literal gods
Showing favor to some and shunning others
and presiding over religious corporations
too big to fail.

May these words, symbols, metaphors and poems
be partial penance for my necessary and unnecessary sins.

Monotheistic Madness

Necessity, they say, is the mother of invention
Religions not excluded
Meaning–making the inventive force
Along with security
For awe-wired fear-filled
Two-legged mammals
Treading a vast terrain
Under a vaster Sky.

Deities and demons were once spied
Everywhere
In nature's glorious gardens
Imaginative helpers and hindrances
Granting Homo sapiens
And theistic religions
A reason to be.

Monotheists later went mad
With claims of being
The one-and-only chosen tribe
(Thrice in succession)
Of the One-and-Only
Including
The possessors and dispensers of
Unchangeable truths
Carved in stone and permanent ink
Promoting narcissism, paranoia, scapegoating.

Attempts to control Monotheistic Madness
By reform and revival
And new spins on ancient texts
Have failed
The divisive disease
Metastasized
Contaminating cultures and politics
And family tables.

How will we ever be one family
When only a few are chosen
When only a few are given

The keys to unlock theistic doors
Where the human imagination
Is held hostage
To psychological complexes
Idealizing out there
The lonely orphans
In here?

The theistic imagination
Requires a do-over
External deities and devils
No longer believable
Nor necessary
Shelf-life long past
Best-by-date faded
Underneath health warnings
To conscious consumers
Of spoiled contents
Dangerous to body and soul.

The monotheistic foundation stone
Of chosen-ness
By a preferential deity
Must be excavated and crushed
Into glass
For psychological mirrors
To view
The multiple chambers
Of the human heart
Housing love and hate

Light and dark
Reflected off the faces of
Heroes and Sheroes and enemies
Human and divine.

Perhaps theism and monotheism
Were necessary stages
Along the dimly lit religious path
And the barely lit religious imagination
Slowly unfolding
Still squinting
To see the dawn
The promised light
That we are
The shining ones
Long awaited
Emerging from the dark unconscious.

May They Rest in Peace

Let us grant our external
Supernatural
Interventionist
Deities and devils
Their well-earned eternal rest
To Mount Olympus or Sinai or Mecca
Or wherever our imagination has so assigned
They labored far too long
At our insistent imploring with

Hands folded in pious prayer
As if to hand over
Our responsibility
For both our glory and gory
By creating a never-ending herd of scapegoats,
Divine and human.

Let us grant our god-men and god-women rest
As well
From declaring holy with magic words
Bread and wine already holy
And Presence
Already always present
And forgiveness not theirs to grant.

Yet may we never rest
From embracing
Our deity-like and devil-like capacities
Long exported
Until the terror-filled trade deficit
Of our own making
Is erased
And human and humane commerce flow freely
Making way for the peace that passes
And surpasses understanding
And small
Literal
Minds.

Psyche/Soul

She a web of wisdom
known and yet-to-be known
Conscious and unconscious
The original
Worldwide web
With unlimited storage space
Never forgetting nor littering
Always recycling
Our mystical inheritance
and legacy
No password needed
except attention.

We are held together in Soul's web
Interconnected, interdependent, inter-are
and entangled
Colorful skeins
for the one tapestry
Archetypal patterns and potentials
Emerging from the depths.

We are children of the cosmos
Origin and parentage beyond knowing
Creator God and Evolution
two of many metaphors
to satisfy our curiosity
to name the unnamable
As nature's meaning-seekers
and meaning-makers.

All matter
including matter considered dark
is alive and animated
A troupe of exotic
Soul dancers
in a long-running performance
inviting our participation
No wall flowers permitted
nor walls.

Soul remains her mystical name
for matters of the heart
While psyche speaks to the
scientific psychological mind
Heart and mind being
two sides of the same
cosmic coin
Kissing cousins to
spiritual and physical
Soul and body
forever wed.

We Are Born Mystics

We are born mystics
Squeezed through the thin place
in the cosmic curtain
Suddenly a lifetime threshold-dweller
between visible and invisible

light and dark
Always on the edge
of the mystical path
Animated and enlivened.

We are born mystics
Long before we are religious
or spiritual
both optional add-ons
Longer still before theism and monotheism
dominated the landscape
and soul-scape
Demanding belief over experience
and tribalism over community
With holy books and holy men
given the last word.

We are born mystics
married to mystery
divorce not possible
Wed to pondering unanswerable questions
Like an unquenchable thirst
in the bar room of life
with spirits everywhere
Housed in beautiful bodies
long before bottles.

We are born mystics
emerging from the pregnant
numinous darkness
into the light of day

Assigned to be and become lights
of consciousness and compassion
our primary vocation
The rent we pay for being alive.

We are born mystics
tethered to the unbreakable sacred umbilical
No redemption needed
save in the small fear-filled
evangelical imagination
infected with Monotheistic Madness.

We are born mystics
destined to be and to become
the conscious deities and devils
long seen in projected guise
Mirroring our longing-filled
body and soul
Waiting for the kairos moment
to tip the cosmic scales
with our grain of incarnated sand
Our unwritten lived creed
our best worship.

Numinous

Numinous . . .
A mystical nod from the gods
Coined by Otto, borrowed by Jung

Cornerstone for his personal and professional
Psychological house
Experiential balm for the
Ailing soul.

Numinous ...
Equal nods to all
Religious or non
Theists, atheists, nones alike
Color and credentials left unchecked
On the border between
Visible and invisible.

Numinous ...
Holy visits
Uninvited, unknown
Unmediated, unmistaken
Unnamable
Symbols, metaphors, and images
Sufficient.

Numinous ...
Activated body and intense emotions
The first responders
Announcing invisible visitors
Bearing gifts
Sometimes desired
Always needed.

Numinous ...
New word for ancient universal experiences
Baptizing low as well as high

Dark as well as light
Flesh as well as spirit
Sacred homes for the
Holy.

Numinous . . .
Holy retrieved from the heavens
Providing muddy shoes
To complement the halo effect
Ordinary moment by moment, by moment
Miracles
The most believable kind.

Numinous . . .
Ordinary mystics invited
To exit their closets
To claim standing place and voice
In the crowded religious marketplace
Selling no dogma or doctrine
Except *I know.*

Numinous . . .
When the gods come a-nodding
On the mystical path less traveled
A humble reciprocal bow
Or seventy times seven
Will suffice
To mark all places and all times as holy.

Mystical Path

A mystical path
May be more desirable for those
Desiring to be more human
Rather than more religious or spiritual
The latter two being detours
On the long journey home
To our common humanity
Our most sacred inheritance.

Religion and spirituality are generally designed
To take one up and away
From the ground of being itself
Machinations to make one fit
For the great Eye in the Sky
An Eye that has gone to sleep
No longer on duty.

That God can no longer help us
No longer hears our prayerful pleas
To do for us
What we must do for ourselves.

That God is no more and never was
His ghost summoned
By those needing to feel special
While arguing over creation myths
And who is in and who is out
And who will be saved in the end
And who will be left out.

Those we have named gods
Were never in the saving business anyway
The only thing lost
Being the creative imagination
Sacrificed to me-my-mine-us
Of tribalism.

We have created problems
Only we can solve or not
Intervening gods having moved on
Leaving us children
The possibility of growing up
Or not
Of being more human
Or less than.

The Road Less Traveled

Two roads diverged into a wood
And Frost took the difference-making one
Followed by psychologist Peck
Both explorers of poetic soul
Leaving trail markers
For future explorers.

That idyllic wood is disappearing fast
To clear-cutting and asphalt
For roads that go
Nowhere faster

And oversized houses for
Oversized egos.

Those once diverging wooded paths
Are now buried
Beneath tons of steel and concrete
In spider webs of ugly twisted art
At converging highways
Replacing the ways of bees and birds
And spiders.

Why must we faithfully execute the command
To multiply, subdue, and dominate
Yet ignore wisdom from the same book
To consider the birds of the air
And the lilies of the field
Who are Nature's
Models of trust?

Our road choices do matter
Do make all the difference
For our Mother
And her offspring
Life and death at stake
In Carson's *Silent Spring*.

Future generations
May well profit from the poet's wisdom
While wondering about the wooded paths
He bespoke
Lost to our lust for progress
And profit.

The way we treat the body of the Earth
Mirrors the way we treat our own flesh
And that of others
And the body politic
As outer so inner and reverse.

Consume more and more
Drill baby drill
Echoes of unconscious treatment
Of Earth
And women
And the feminine in all of us.

What trail markers are we leaving
For future generations
Should there be some
To consider diverging paths?

The City of More

Consult any western atlas or GPS
(Or simply ask Siri)
For directions to the City of More
A superhighway with soul left languishing
In two miles of ditches
For every mile of asphalt
Ditches filled with tear-stained adult toys
Touted by consumer priests
As missing pieces

To the happiness puzzles
Of vulnerable love-longing
Love-lonely humans.

Surely more is always better
Along with bigger and higher
And being great again.

How dare that mystical rabbi
Propose otherwise
That less is more
The first shall be last
And vice versa
That the greatest are servants of all?

How dare he!
What was that homeless
Itinerant mystic smoking
Declaring happy are the humble
Poor in spirit peacemakers?

What did he know
He who had only twelve followers
On his Twitter account?

Is the rapidly expanding City of More
A shining light to the nations
Or a flickering diminishing candle
On the edge of darkness?

Is the City of More
A beacon for freedom and justice
And equality for all
Or only for the well-connected
Who can afford health care?

Is the City of More
Capitalism's success
Or cannibalism's delight
Earth's honor or soul's sorrow?

Each of us is a
Judge and jury of one
Considering our verdict
In the City of More.

In the season of Covid-19
The highways to the City of More
Were less traveled
Except for the virtual ones
The skies were bluer
The air was cleaner
The birds seemed to be rejoicing
While we pondered possible meanings.

Might it be that the expansion of
Soul
Requires less and less
And fewer and fewer
More subtraction than addition?

Jesus

Down-to-earth, embodied, mystical teacher
Nature's son, Nature's friend, and Nature's voice
Employing divinity-laden soil and seed
Flowers and birds
Spit, salt, and tears
As props for the long running human drama
Played out on Nature's stage
Inviting suspended belief.

How lonely he now must be
A one-and-only savior
Exiled by creedal-crazed apostles
To a metallic three-seated
Air traffic control tower
To contemplate an unnecessary
Second Coming
And role of final judge
He decried the first time around.

How sad he must now be
His elevation to sanitized divine status
Far from humans and humus he held dear
As if his body, and ours, not sacred enough
Nor his parents' sexual intimacy
Sufficiently holy for birthing
Requiring spiritualization
To cover ancient shame.

Was his creedal exile an eternal reward
Or a sentence to irrelevancy
His life story reduced
To a few unbelievable sentences
Parroted weekly in the tribal echo chamber
Simply marking the end of the printed order
Before departing
Worship completed.

Perhaps those apostles like us
Were addressing their own unconscious
Hopes and fears and longings
For a far-off reality
Already in their/our midst
Awaiting incarnation
Our own lived creedal do-over
Saving Jesus
From his long exile.

Mary

Exalted above all women
Yet hidden for eternity
Behind a prophylactic veil
Declaring human body and flesh
And sexuality
Tainted by Augustinian original sin
Birthing guilt and shame
For the ages.

One wonders if she might have preferred
Her lowly human estate
Over a spiritualized and desexualized
Dehumanized elevation
Untouchable by ordinary women and men
Except by counting prayer beads
Or viewing iconic images
Of mother and child.

Why do men then and now
Religious or otherwise
Prefer their feminine nature in projected forms
Safely out there at arms' distance
Idealized or demonized
Escaping the risky and vulnerable
Tissue of sacred body
And tender solace of soul?

When the angel next visits Mary
Imploring her willingness to birth divinity
She may well decline
Preferring to be a human mother
For a human son
Rich in body and soul
Mind and imagination
Content with an ordinary miracle.

Joseph

Poor father Joseph
Almost written out of the script
Not privy to Mary's angelic contract
Left pondering his earthly role
And the sufficiency of his seed
While Mary pondered her
Heavenly impregnation
Both wondering why me?

He was there at the birthing
Saving his infant son
Thanks to the appearance of a dream
Only to disappear from the family narrative
Replaced by a heavenly Father
Whose business his precocious son
Needed to be about with
The Temple priests.

Was he proud of his son's holy business
With the invisible world
Or did he desire him in the family trade
Building visible things
Or was he simply satisfied
That he helped
To build his son's character?

History remains uneven
Mother Mary granted headlines
And art and songs

And sainthood
And Father Joseph a little more than a footnote
To the greatest story
Ever told
About the boy *he* fathered.

Upon hearing their mythologized biographies
Touting virginity and divine intercourse
Their reproductive prime now long past
Joseph looked at Mary lovingly
While a slow sheepish
Knowing grin
Covered his wise
Wrinkled countenance.

I Know

Having taken leave of the
back porch of the Church
and my ancestral religious tribe
To scout out their possible futures
and my uncertain one
My scouting report is dire
reminiscent of the Old One
There is a new land just over the horizon
though not the one Promised to Moses
Giants nevertheless
Ancient psychic fears and prejudices
hidden beneath wishful god-talk

ignored for centuries
We must stare them down
eye to eye
the flesh-eating and Earth-eating monsters
Standing in the path ahead
for our sacred species
and our holy humus.

Scouting reports to the faithful
evoke challenging questions about faith
Well, do you still believe in God
Have you lost your faith?

Carefully consulting my deep-down knowing
birthed from rock-solid experience and conviction
revised by divine doubts
My response echoes Jung
facing the same question near his end
I do not need to believe
I know!

What did he know
that mystic
in psychological garb
What do I know
What do you know?

I know that I am
though I do not know
where I was before
nor where or how I will be after.

I know that life is full of mysteries
those we have named gods and goddesses
no less so

I know that soul is as real as brain
the invisible as real as visible
That I am apprehended
by uncomprehended powers and presences
and plots and patterns
Who entangle me
in the net of unknowing.

I know that I am being sought
though I do not see my pursuers
nor clearly their intent
That I am also the one seeking
the seekers
A mutual game of hide and seek
forever playing out
in the meadows of my mind.

I know that faith and trust are identical twins
often confused with beliefs
that have other parentage
That beliefs breed mistrust of those
who believe differently
or not at all

I know that guarded beliefs
shrink the imaginative soul
While trust releases

the religious prisoners
That beliefs can change
and must
lest religious word-idols
slay us all.

I know that trust is delicate and hardy
like the first cry
announcing our arrival
on this spinning top
and our final sigh at the end
The trust of breath and gravity
being our first and last
faith-filled acts
in this numinous Cosmos.

I know that we create our gods
from numinous experiences
not of our making
That we create gods
who in turn create us
and hopefully save us
from ourselves
That devils are created likewise
from dark shadowlands
projected onto the faces
of those we hate or fear.

I know that all religious dogma
is necessary subjective fiction
always needing a revised sequel
That all sacred texts are human words

about the gods we create
That our god-naming and religion-making
are necessary industries
to employ the human imagination.

I know that our visible Earth
is more precious
than a hoped-for heaven
That our at-one-ment with all
more precious than
atonement for a few
And if there is something like salvation
it will be for all
or none.

I know that I know very little
in the larger scheme of things
That I remain a final puzzle to myself
and others
Prompting the conclusion
to this trust-filled litany
But, then, what do I know
And you?

Why?

Why have we spent centuries
building religious highways to heaven
When Nature's numinous paths
lead directly Home?

Why must we look for miracles
from external supernatural deities
When Nature's internal miracles
are super enough?

Why do we invest
in the industries of remote deities
to save us
Rather than investing in
honest self-reflection
to save ourselves from ourselves?

Why do we consider
walking on water
or changing water into wine
More miraculous
than our next breath
that repeats its miracle
fifteen to twenty times
every minute?

O Christians, why do we continue to spill blood
in the name of the one
whose spilled blood
was supposedly spilled for all
And why are we so enamored
with drinking symbolic blood
more than ridding our world
of blood-spilling weapons?

Why do we continue to elevate
beliefs over trust

creed over character
skin color over soul
men over women
masculine over feminine
miracles over mystery
and Bronze-age men
and their books
over common sense?

Why is sex considered so dirty
so shameful
when each of us is its joyful
outcome?

Why do we fight so tenaciously
for our babies in the womb
Yet so eagerly send our babies
to fight and kill other babies
Who happen to be born
from wombs of the same flesh
but with different names?

Why does it take a lifetime
to come home to ourselves
When we live so close?

And the most puzzling question of all
why do I suppose
I see more clearly than most
the important issues
facing our world and our species?

Epitaph

I am out there
Naked before the Cosmos
The Great Mystery
With neither god-shield
Nor religion-shield
For protection.

All has been stripped away
Or tossed aside
Except my own inner contradictions
As I await the consequences of
Living religiously naked.

There is no going back
Nor can I see ahead
I stand vulnerable
Awaiting lightening
Or enlightenment
Or both or neither.

My consolation is the strange freedom
That comes with knowing
I made my pilgrimage
I cast my lot
I made my bet
Never sure if I won or lost
But convinced I could do no other.

ACKNOWLEDGEMENTS

For me, writing is very hard work. It takes daily discipline, dedication, multiple starts and stops, and a large supply of patience. Publishing my writing with Chiron Publications, however, has been relatively easy. I would say it has been a delight, a joy! I am grateful to the professional and personable Chiron staff for making it so.

I send special appreciation to Steve Buser, M.D., Jennifer Fitzerald, and a host of readers and artists who remain unseen, yet greatly appreciated. Your dedication to your soulful work continues to enrich the Jungian community and contributes to a more hospitable world. Thank you!

SOURCES CITED

Baring, Anne. (2020) *The Dream of the Cosmos, A Quest for Soul,* Dorset, England: Archive Publishing.

Barrows, Anita and Macy, Joanna. (Trans.). (1996) *Rilke's Book of Hours: Love Poems to God,* New York: Riverhead Books.

Berry, Thomas. (1988) *The Dream of the Earth,* Berkeley, CA: Counterpoint.

----- (2006) *Evening Thoughts,* Berekely, CA: Counterpoint.

Bly, Robert. (Trans.). (1981) *Selected Poems of Rainer Maria Rilke,* New York: Harper & Row.

Borg, Marcus. (2006) *Jesus,* New York: HarperCollins.

Delio, Ilia. (2023) *The Not-Yet God: Carl Jung, Teilhard de Chardin and the Relational Whole,* Maryknoll, NY: Orbis Books.

Hollis, James. (1995) *Tracking the Gods: The Place of Myth in Modern Life,* Toronto, Canada: Inner City Books.

----- (2003) *On This Journey We Call Our Lives,* Toronto, Canada: Inner City Books.

----- (2020) *Living Between Worlds: Finding Personal Resilience in Changing Times,* Boulder, CO: Sounds True.

----- (2025) *Living With Borrowed Dust: Reflections on Life, Love, and Other Grievances,* Boulder, CO: Sounds True.

Jacobi, Jolande. (1971) *Complex, Archetype, Symbol: In the Psychology of C.G. Jung,* Princeton, NJ: Princeton University Press.

Jung, C. G. (1932) "Psychotherapists or the Clergy," *Psychology and Religion: West and East, Collected Works, Volume 11,* Princeton, NJ: Princeton University Press.

----- (1943) "The Psychic Nature of the Alchemical Work," *Psychology and Alchemy, Collected Works, Volume 12,* Princeton, NJ: Princeton University Press.

----- (1945b) Letter to P. W. Martin, 20 August 1945, in G. Adler and A. Jaffe (eds) *C. G. Jung Letters, Volume 1, 1906-1950,* Princeton, NJ: Princeton University Press.

----- *(*1946*)* "On The Nature of the Psyche," *The Structure and Dynamics of the Psyche, Collected Works, Volume 8,* Princeton, NJ: Princeton University Press.

----- (1956) *Symbols of Transformation, Volume 5,* Princeton, NJ: Princeton University Press.

----- (1957) Letter to Miss Roswitha, 17 August 1957, in G. Adler and A. Jaffe (eds) *C. G. Jung Letters, Volume 2, 1951-1961,* Princeton, NJ: Princeton University Press.

----- (1958a) "Jung and Religious Belief," *The Symbolic Life, Collected Works, Volume 18,* Princeton, NJ: Princeton University Press.

----- (1958b) "Healing the Split," *The Symbolic Life, Collected Works, Volume 18,* Princeton, NJ: Princeton University Press.

----- (1958c) "Psychology and Religion," *Psychology and Religion: West and East, Volume 11,* Princeton, NJ: Princeton University Press.

----- (1959) Letter to M. Leonard, 5 December 1959 in G. Adler and A. Jaffe (eds.) *C. G. Jung Letters, Volume 2, 1951-1961,* Princeton, NJ: Princeton University Press.

----- (1959a) "The Shadow," *Aion, Collected Works, Volume 9ii,* Princeton, NJ: Princeton University Press.

----- (1960) "General Aspects of Dream Psychology," *The Structure and Dynamics of the Psyche, Collected Works, Volume 8,* Princeton, NJ: Princeton University Press.

----- (1963) "The Conjunction," *Mysterium Coniunctionis, Collected Works, Volume 14,* Princeton, NJ: Princeton University Press.

----- (1964a) "After the Catastrophe," *Civilization In Transition, Collected Works, Volume 10,* Princeton, NJ: Princeton University Press.

----- (1964b) "The Fight with the Shadow," *Civilization in Transition, Collected Works, Volume 10,* Princeton, NJ: Princeton University Press.

----- *(1965) Memories, Dreams, Reflections,* A. Jaffe (ed.), New York, NY: Vintage, Random House.

----- (1967) *Alchemical Studies, Collected Works, Volume 13,* Princeton, NJ: Princeton University Press.

----- (1977) *C. G. Jung Speaking, Interviews and Encounters,* William McGuire and R. F. C. Hull (eds), Bollingen Series XCV11, Princeton, NJ: Princeton University Press.

Keltner, Dacher. (2024) *Awe: The New Science of Everyday Wonder and How It Can Transform Your Life,* New York: Penguin Books.

Lerner, Alan Jay. (1956) "Show Me," lyrics from *My Fair Lady,* Broadway premier March 15, 1956, http://warnerbros.fandom.com.

Macy, Joanna. (2020) *A Wild Love for the World,* Boulder, CO: Shambhala Publications.

Oliver, Mary. (1992) "A Summer Day," *New and Selected Poems,* Boston: Beacon Press.

Stein, Murray. (2017) *Outside, Inside, and All Around and Other Essays in Jungian Psychology,* Asheville, NC: Chiron Publications.

Swimme, Brian. (2022) *Cosmogenesis,* Berkeley, CA: Counterpoint.

Tacey, David. (2020) *The Postsecular Sacred: Jung, Soul and Meaning in an Age of Change,* New York: Routledge.

Tagore, Rabindranath. (2020) *What Wants to Come Through Me Now,* Coleman Barks (Trans), Louisville, KY: Fons Vitae.

Walcott, Derek. (1986) *Collected Poems 1948-1984,* New York: Farrar, Strauss, and Giroux.

Wilson, Edward O. (2014) *The Meaning of Human Existence,* New York: Liveright Publishing.

Wright, Jerry R. (2018) *Reimagining* God *and Religion*: *Essays for the Psychologically Minded,* Asheville, NC: Chiron Publications.

----- (2021) *A Mystical Path Less Traveled: A Jungian Psychological Perspective,* Asheville, NC: Chiron Publications.

www.ingramcontent.com/pod-product-compliance
Lightning Source LLC
LaVergne TN
LVHW090412210926
848480LV00002B/542
9781685036638